OUR
COLLECTIVE
CONTRIBUTION
TO THE
DECADENCE
IN
NIGERIA

CHRISTINE
UMOEKEREKA
(SHUTTI)

OUR COLLECTIVE CONTRIBUTION
TO THE DECADENCE IN NIGERIA

Published by Christine Umoekereka (Shutti), Edmonton, Canada

ISBN:
   Paperback 978-1-77354-343-7
   ebook 978-1-77354-344-4

Publication assistance and digital printing in Canada by

PAGEMASTER
PUBLISHING
PageMaster.ca

ACKNOWLEDGEMENTS

Special thanks for research assistance to:

Emmanuel James Umoekereka

Pastor Michael Success

and Francis Ojaloma

CONTENTS

NIGERIA WILL TRIUMPH AGAIN

Nigeria glory can be restored if we all
collectively think and act accordingly
with morals, love, kindness, etc.
towards each other,
towards our country,
towards developing the country.

TOGETHER WE CAN DO IT

INTRODUCTION

Over the years, I have listened to the yearnings of many people for a better Nigeria. I am one of them. While we have much work to do, this publication explains in varying divine ways our need for God's intervention in the polity.

This piece of literature is a sterling testament to our collective contributions and the thought-provoking, shared guilt that must be felt by all, but that ultimately might lead Nigeria to victory. When people are frustrated about a project or an enterprise, they champion it by applying Lean Methodology. This volume seeks to outline the collective blame—and therefore the collective realization—that we all can play a part in fixing the rot.

Martin Luther King Jr. declared in his sound, unending resolve that, "Our lives begin to end the day we become silent about things that matter," and he added that, "Darkness cannot drive out darkness, only light can do that" (KeepInspiring.me. n.d.).

This concept has worked for other countries, including Canada where I live and practice as a Registered Nurse. In this part of the globe, everything seems to work accordingly. The same ideation can factually be employed in Nigeria. Looking back on the good old days when Nigeria was a bride of the nations—what went wrong? This book examines all of that.

Based on the perennial and recurrent challenges, every area of our national life has been carefully examined in this book in an attempt to find a solution. Remember—complex problems, collective amnesia, malaise, and deprivation are not solvable by declaring them simple, but rather through collective reasoning.

Before we proceed, let us consider two questions that have the same answer:

1.   What makes up a nation?
     a.   the people
     b.   the government

2.   In the absence of war and natural disasters, et cetera, what other factors could be responsible for the fall of a nation?
     a.   the people
     b.   the government

As previously stated, the above questions have one and the same answer: the "a" option. Without mincing words, it is the people that make up a nation, as well as the functional operators of every institution of government, and by their attitudes, orientations, and perceptions, the nation either rises or falls. As fundamentally necessary as this is to take into account, we must understand that patriotism and citizenship provide a solid foundation for national growth and cohesion.

For many years, I have dealt with people who understand that citizenship is about a sense of nationhood. With this shared, national understanding, Canada, like many prosperous nations, has been able to build a reputation through its citizens' commitment to upholding core beliefs, values, and principles.

Back home in Nigeria, it is different and disheartening. A good number of people have lost faith in the country based on our incorrect orientation, socio-political socialization, bad parenting, and cultural transmission. Regrettably, these vices have led to the visible and moral decadence of the present generation who is considered to be the strength and hope for the future. This is a great cause of concern of mine, and our statement of the problem.

We have also come to this hallowed spot to remind Nigerians of the fierce urgency of now. This is no time to engage in the luxury of cooling off or to take the tranquilizing drug of gradualism. Now is the time to make possible the promises of democracy.

The fact remains that life is usually hard for the common populace in the streets of every developing country. It is, however, not enough reason to tolerate a society, community, or a nation polluted by corruption, avarice, nepotism, structural defects, lack of government accountability, and relative deprivations.

The future of our country, and the destiny of our children and our children's children, is in dire danger if we continue to plunder it as we have been doing by allowing the embezzling of public funds to continue unabated at all tiers of government. A storm is about to destroy the entire nation.

This is the narrative we seek to change about Nigeria, a situation where criminal negligence continues to occupy centre stage in national and street affairs. The rat race becomes even more sinister and intense, affecting all fabrics of our collective beings, including the youth who are the most important resource for future economic and national growth.

Worst of all, there is a common social streak of honouring and recognizing the dubious and doubtful wealth of people without asking and investigating how it came about. This has encouraged fraudulent and deviant behaviour in our youth.

None of us is entirely blameless in this matter. The truth is that no building can stand without a firm foundation; neither can a nation. It is time to stop the blame game and face the reality that is our collective guilt. We will not be able to get it right as a nation until we understand that our personal lives shape and control our national life, and therefore our individual attitudes determine our collective growth.

Nigerians must be patriotic enough to abide by the codes of conduct based on the rule of law. While we admit there are many bad eggs in government, we will not accept that the real reasons behind national growth retardation and decay in the country must linger. If we must overcome the cancer worm militating against our national prosperity, each individual has to look inward, examine themselves, examine their consciences, and take conscious steps toward reorganizing, reorienting, reengineering their personal value system.

As a people, what we seriously need are changes in the social, political, and economic structures of our society. We accept that this would be a huge, hard fight, but if we want to win, we are going to have to swallow our greed, selfishness, and tribalistic tendencies and follow the winning ways of those who have walked this path and achieved success. We also have to stop pointing fingers, because this is a collective problem that requires a collective solution. Let anyone with a clean conscience in Nigeria come out to say, "I am clean," and prove his or her clean conscience.

Consider the biblical account recorded in John 8:4-10:

> "4...and said to Jesus, "Teacher, this woman was caught in the act of adultery. 5 In the Law Moses commanded us to stone such women. Now what do you say?" 6 They were using this question as a trap, in order to have a basis for accusing him.

> But Jesus bent down and started to write on the ground with his finger. 7 When they kept on questioning him, he straightened up and said to them, "Let any one of you who is without sin be the first to throw a stone at her." 8 Again he stooped down and wrote on the ground.

[9] At this, those who heard began to go away one at a time, the older ones first, until only Jesus was left, with the woman still standing there. [10] Jesus straightened up and asked her, "Woman, where are they? Has no one condemned you?"

[11] "No one, sir," she said.

"Then neither do I condemn you," Jesus declared. "Go now and leave your life of sin" (John 8:4-11 NIV n.d.).

The accused woman is the government. The accusers are the CITIZENS who refuse to judge their own faults and contributions to the national calamity. Similarly, "The pot is calling the kettle black." This means that our people are criticizing our president for a fault they themselves have collectively contributed to—the damage to our nation:

- Our projected bad image abroad
- The decline in education
- The miscarriage of justice
- The commercialization of the gospel
- The truncation of democratic tenets
- The lack of accountability in government
- The spate of kidnappings, domination, and marginalization of others
- Insecurity in our land
- Authoritarianism in our nascent democracy
- Daily recorded gender-based violence

And yet, in the midst of all of these, we believe in the Nigerian dream.

Evolving from a passion to see a better Nigeria, we have put together this insightful and analytical book. This volume focuses on the Nigerian society, touching on the real issues facing us as a people and pointing at our character and the possible ways to navigate out from our collective contributions to the decadence.

The following images are horrific and appalling. It's disheartening to see Nigeria in this way. These are essentials that have been neglected for many years and that need immediate fixing. To the government appointees and political leaders who have stolen billions of dollars and left our country in this tragic state, what do you have to say for yourselves?

Fakoyelo O. (2019, August 13). "AfcFTA under threat of poor power supply at TCN MD proffers solution." Nairmetrics.

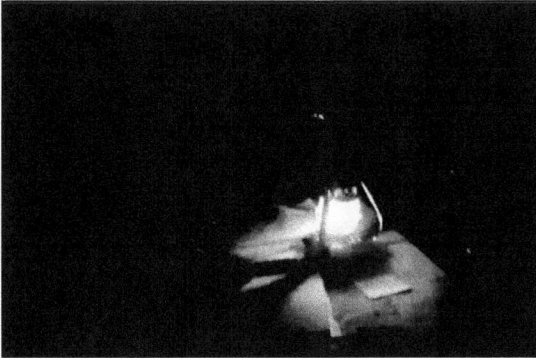

Olawoyin, Oladeinde. (2018, January 3). Nigeria experiences total power outage across country. Premium Times.

Muoh, Obinna F. (2016 July 14). "When 95 million Nigerians are living without electricity something needs to change." Business Insider.

Yohanna I. (2020, July 14). "Electricity tariff increase'll not affect poor consumers- NERC". Voice of Liberty.

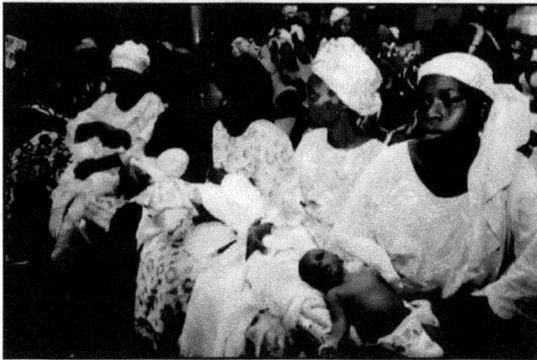

Adesokan O (2020, January 7) "Surgery by candle light: Hospitals in Nigeria suffer losing power and staff" Guardian News.

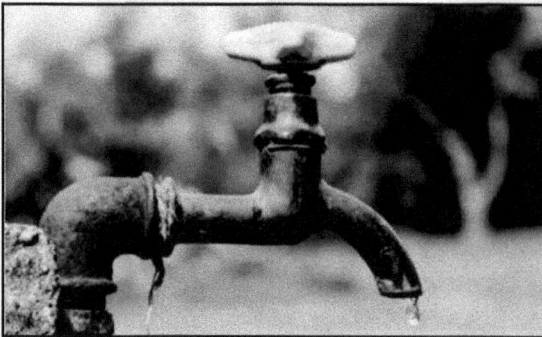

Adelagun O, (2021 June 23) "less than 40% of Lagos residents has access to water –Governor." Premium Times.

Njoku B, Ndaji S & Babalola E. (2017 August 5) "Inside world of people who live in dump sites". Vanguard News.

Omiko A & Akinfenwa G. (2021, July 18). "A nation in search of lasting solution to perennial flooding." Guardian Sunday magazine.

Thisday News. (2018 Nov 28) "Bad road threatens completion of #3.5bn baro River port in Niger state".

Akoni O. (2019, October 21) "Flood sack Lagos,Ogun boarder residents after heavy downpour". Vanguard News.

Babarinsa D. (2019, October 10). "Bad road paved with good intentions". Guardian Opinion.

Vanguard News.(2017, Dec 6) "why many companies would close shops if Apapa roads remain bad.- OPS".

CHAPTER 1

FAMILY SYSTEMS

How are we supposed to have a change in Nigeria when the root of the problem plaguing the country is still lingering in the family system, in our communities, and in our society at large?

At the early stage of human development, what we see, hear, and learn, how we are treated, and how we are spoken to can have a positive or a negative impact on our development. The interaction and socialization patterns determine the mindsets in the process of growth.

Parental behaviour has a strong effect on the social, cultural, and psychological aspects of child development. When a child is growing up, they rely on their family and significant others for detailed information about society. From all that is learned, the child develops a sense of their identity; this identity will be carried with them into adulthood.

If a child grows up seeing that all their parents care about is money, then they will grow up with this negative reinforcement, believing money is the only thing of value.

There is a popular saying in Nigeria: "A child who brings money home commands the respect of his parents. A child who has no money will experience discrimination and suffer rejection and humiliation by his parents and siblings."

The accomplishments of such children are often not celebrated—they are relegated by the parents and deemed as insignificant. The child's worth is reduced to nothing because the parents are too focused on money. The attitudes of some of these parents have caused the child to struggle by living a life of competition and being plagued by the determination to be successful at any cost. They will strive for and do anything that will bring the highest earnings at any cost, even at the expense of our beloved nation and other citizens' inconveniences—they just don't care.

I have seen it firsthand in some families. The only child the parents call often is the one who brings food to the table, while the other children who are still struggling to make a life for themselves are neglected. As a result, those excluded children are driven into loneliness, isolation, desperation, depression, gangs, drugs, prostitution, robbery, kidnapping, and all manner of detrimental behaviours.

A lot of pressure is placed on our Nigerian children, even from before birth. From conception, some of our Nigerians have already determined the unborn child's future—to become a medical doctor, a lawyer, an accountant, a governor, an engineer, etc. Why? Because these professions are seen as the ones that are most profitable, superior, and prestigious. From the time they are born, children are brainwashed into thinking they have to pursue these specific careers so they can make their families proud and make the most money. Children adopt these radical beliefs from their parents.

In Nigerian society, almost everyone is expected to have big house, multiple cars, and fancy clothes and accessories because that is the only way to be acknowledged and respected among family, friends, community, and society at large.

This societal doctrine has created an incessant need for a luxurious lifestyle and impregnates a rivalry among our people—children and adults alike. However, with poverty and with the approximately 60% unemployment rate in the country, most Nigerian children don't have the legitimate means to accomplish these prestigious goals, so they have to resort to criminal acts such as kidnapping and robbery, corruption, dishonest acts, fraudulent acts, and the like in order to obtain wealth at the cost of the masses.

Wealth superiority and ascendancy are all youth are taught to care about, even at the expense of their morality. This mentality needs to change. No child should have to endure this kind of pressure to become something that they are not, all for the sake of wealth. People who do something just because external factors are forcing them to do it will fail. We cannot allow our younger generation to conform to what society and our families want them to be. We cannot allow for the potential of our younger generation to be stripped away because our collective goal has become about making the most affluence.

Human beings are created to perform all different kinds of functions. We cannot all be lawyers, doctors, accountants, governors, politicians, pastors, etc. We need farmers to supply the food on our tables. We need architects and construction workers to build and design better houses, schools, and hospitals for our communities. If the children are all striving for the same occupations (i.e., a medical doctor), other areas of Nigerian society will be lacking substantially with huge consequences. All individuals aren't made to fit into the same mould, and we need to stop forcing our children into believing that their options are so limited. It stunts their growth and diminishes their self-worth, and it impedes the economy.

Furthermore, to be a successful nation, we all have to take on different tasks so that the various roles of a society are fulfilled.

Another negative effect of family and community pressures to acquire wealth and become rich is that no one in Nigeria wants to work hard, be patient, or wait for their time to have money anymore—they just want to make money as quickly as possible and often in a dubious way.

The concept of hard work, morals, and ethical values has become completely invaluable to the nation.

I am not an exception to the above. I came from a family who only cared about wealth, superiority, discrimination, humiliation, and value according to your wealth. Hence, rivalry to keep other siblings down from rising to wealth occurs in order to avoid losing prestige, superiority, or admiration. Just like the nation is broken and divided, this has affected my family too: destroyed our love, support, and dragged us to the pit. Instead of rising, we are falling.

From a very young age, I knew that the plan my parents had for my life was not going to lead me to where I wanted to be or make me happy. I have a passion for caring, so I left Nigeria in my early twenties to seek after my own career—not what they planned for me or wanted me to do. So, I went to university to get a degree in nursing, which is my passion. Guess what? I am so happy and content; I wouldn't want to do anything different. This is what I was meant to be.

Some years ago, a childhood friend of mine told me that going to nursing school is a twenty-year fruitless journey. She said this because she was a victim of the indoctrination that going to school is part of the long process to be wealthy.

I was told it was pointless. Getting money as fast as you can was the way you could live that glorious, luxury lifestyle, and it should be my main focus. In Nigeria, people don't respect you if you have worked hard for the money you have; they only respect you if you're wearing a designer watch and carrying around a designer handbag. However, today I am a Registered Nurse, and I am content with the life I have made for myself. If I had taken a shorter route just so I could make fast money, it might have resulted in me ending up with the wrong crowds and committing criminal acts much like what we see with some of our Nigerians today.

What we need to understand in order for our nation to get better is that having a luxurious life does not always signify happiness or betterment.

This striving for instant gratification has impeded the economic growth of Nigeria, solidifies our name abroad as number-one fraudsters, impedes foreign investments that in return stunts economic growth, and impedes our productivity in the country. This is contributing to our economic decline as well.

Even worse is the trend of older generations and parents staying longer in their current jobs and even moving from one job to another. For example, politicians are refusing to give up their seats in the government, which hinders the younger generation from being able to take part. This is detrimental because older politicians are depriving our younger generation of an opportunity to be independent, to fend for themselves, to learn skills, and to avoid unemployment.

Worst of all, the nation's money earmarked for the development of our country and the development of our children's future has been badly mismanaged. The majority is being pocketed and used for selfish and personal purposes. I do not believe the Nigerians that are participating in such acts realize the profound effects and impacts this will have on their children's children in the future. If you look around now, it's already happening to your children, no doubt.

As a result, most of our young graduates are jobless, frustrated, and feeling hopeless. As parents, we have failed them. As a community, we have failed them. As a nation, we have failed our children due to our grasping, greediness, and ego. It is our job to provide for our children and ensure them a stable future.

I hope we are all learning lessons from these facts. I hope now that we can all see the need for luxurious lifestyles has caused the degradation of our entire country. The burden of it has now been placed on our children's shoulders, and their children's shoulders. We need to adopt and emulate a different mentality, one that will enable us to be able to pass on an inheritance to future generations.

Nigeria is an amazing country. It is our home, and we can restore it back to its glory. But we must do it together—collectively is the key.

The president alone cannot fix all these messes that are afflicting our nation and have eaten deep into the flesh of our country. To restore our country, we need cooperative efforts from all Nigerian citizens.

Much like the African proverb, "It takes a village to raise a child," it will take all of our contributions and efforts to revive Nigeria and make it the great country it once was.

We can do it; however, we have to cooperate and work collectively with one love to build our nation.

The disaster that is about to hit our economy will affect us all—it's just around the corner.

As stated by Abraham Lincoln (1858), "*A house divided against itself cannot stand*" (KeepInspiring.me n.d.). Similarly, a nation divided against itself will not progress and will fail as nation, as we are seeing in Nigeria today.

At the beginning, the rich were flourishing in Nigeria, while the poor were feeling the impact of the economy. In Nigeria today, the people who were once rich are now feeling the same impact of the economy as the poor. I am sure we will all agree or are seeing it, as it's gradually affecting all. We all have no food because we neglected the agriculture industry. We all have to drive on fractured and fragmented roads and endure inadequate healthcare and education because the government funds have been selfishly spent elsewhere or diverted to personal use.

In the case of the poor, these circumstances may be worse for them. However, we are all going to suffer so much worse as time goes on if we do not start making changes in Nigeria now.

It is very pathetic to see the state that Nigeria is in.

As a proud Nigerian, I know the potential this country has to be a great nation, and it is disheartening to know that the rest of the world sees us as just a poor, underdeveloped, and corrupt country. A well-organized and well-managed Nigeria would not be described like this. Nigeria's wealth bypasses the wealth of some of the more developed countries. Yet, we still seek aid from these countries. What a humiliation this is to us.

It is awful to imagine that in the twenty-first century, Nigeria fails to provide its citizens with an affordable and quality standard education. Those individuals grasping and pocketing huge sums of Nigerian wealth for luxurious lifestyles and for superiority from the government are hurting themselves indirectly and their generations to come. If you don't create jobs today, your children will not have jobs tomorrow and will be unemployed. Therefore, unemployment is increasing, and it creates more poverty in our country.

This is not the time to fight. This is the time to work together. Fights will break us more and worsen the nation.

This is also not the time to seek a change—a change is not the answer.

Our answer is a change in character in our home, community, and in our society at large. We are the problem and the cause of our Nigerian predicament today. Hence, I make an emotional appeal to you all to reflect on your individual self and the consequences your actions have caused.

CHAPTER 2

CITIZENS' ATTITUDE TOWARDS NATIONAL DEVELOPMENT

Sometimes when things go wrong, one of the ways to resolve the issue is to take a step back in order to appraise or think about what went wrong. This intervention enables people to walk through the situation in a reasonable way so as to find a positive solution and to avoid repeating the same mistake.

I think it is time we pause and collectively go back to where it all started. We cannot "be stuck in the mud forever." It's time to challenge the status quo!

So how do we get out from under this perceived helplessness?

We can get started by a change in the attitude of our inherent, nonchalant character.

Character, like integrity, may determine the rise or the fall of any nation, people, family, or community. Character is the inherent combination of complex attributes that determine a person's moral and ethical actions and reactions, hence the alignment of citizenship as a panacea to national development. It can also determine in very decisive ways the collapse and decay of any nation.

Permit me to digress a little. A certain man met a king and told him a story of how two men in a certain town got their result based on behaviour output. One was rich, the other poor. The rich man owned a great many sheep and cattle. The poor man owned nothing but one little lamb that he had bought and raised. That little lamb grew up with his children, and he was emotionally attached to the lamb that he cuddled in his arms like a daughter. One day, a guest arrived at the home of the rich man, but instead of killing from his own stock, he greedily took the poor man's lamb and killed it to prepare a table for his guest.

Upon hearing the sad story, the king was furious at the rich man, saying, "Surely, any man that does such a thing deserves to die. He must make restitution by paying four lambs to the poor man in place of the one that was unjustifiably taken. He acted with no moral backbone. He showed no pity." (Translation: QUICK JUDGMENT ON OTHERS WITHOUT EXAMINING OURSELVES.)

Then, the storyteller and conscience-bearer turned to the king and said, "You are the man! God gave you all that you ever needed in life. He gave you many riches and women, but you took away the only wife the poor servant had, and for fear of been exposed, you killed your servant." (Translation: CONSEQUENCES OF BAD ACTIONS.)

And the man said to the king, "This is a righteous word from God Almighty to you. Because of what you have done, I will cause your own household to rebel against you. I will give your wives to other men before your very eyes. You did it secretly, but I will expose your shame and reproach openly."

Sometimes, we need to judge and examine ourselves before judging and pointing accusing fingers at others.

One of the major reasons Nigeria has fallen behind is due to the unpatriotic alignment of the citizens to national priority. Our fingers are all on the government without realizing that we are collectively the government. Everybody is blaming the three tiers of government—the executive, judiciary, and legislative.

I was in a car somewhere in the Abuja metropolis in Nigeria, and there was a certain young man in the car. I believe it was the driver who asked the young man a question, saying, "If you were the president of Nigeria today, what would you do?" The young man laughed and responded, "I would steal a lot of money, open companies, fly my family abroad."

Oh! I was shocked to my bones. I then realized why Nigeria is where it is today. No people-oriented growth, no industries, no development. Our conscience is comatose. Now, if you were to vote this kind of young man into power, he would destroy Nigeria even more. My greatest worry is that the youth, whose strength determines the future, has had this kind of mentality and character mortgaged. With this kind of mindset, how will the nation develop?

I am a Nigerian, despite living in Canada. I have seen the attitudes of many Nigerians in different climates of corruptibility. Now, and only now, have l understood the awful dimension of our moral corruptibility.

In addition, I was passing through a pedestrian bridge put in place for the safety of Nigerians. The government had placed a barricade along the highway so that the citizens could use the walkway bridge, due to past accidents recorded on the expressway. However, a lot of our people wanted a shortcut and did not want to walk across the overhead bridge, and as a result, destroyed the barricades the government had spent billions of naira to put in place for their own safety. Nigerians do not want to go through any stress, so climbing pedestrian bridges is hard work for them. Hence, they prefer crossing the highway at the risk of their own lives. These are the attitudes of many of my fellow Nigerians. We are always looking for the shorter route. Our character is one of the contributing factors responsible for the decadence in Nigeria.

The government set up a structure for its citizens and put some of these citizens in that office to oversee the system. Many willingly commercialize the roles the government has placed on their shoulders. To be clear, for example, I went to do a particular registration that the government had made free for all Nigerians, but some people monetized this registration. If they did not receive money in the form of bribes or incentives, they would practically abandon your application indefinitely. But if they received incentives, even the boss would attend to you as fast as possible.

It is a sad and unfair injustice in a supposed democracy. It ought not to be so. The irony and shame on our national psyche are the open avenue to heap all blame on the government for everything.

Yes, our Nigerian government seems to have failed in terms of accountability and failure to provide a level playing field. Nonetheless, we collectively carry most of the blame in our various positions of trust. Even when citizens are caught red-handed for violating the code of conduct, the judiciary seems willing in more ways than one to allow the rule of law to stand on its head. They will still tell you, "No be government cause am?" which is Nigerian slang and translates literally to that it is the fault of government. Oh? Really!

Nevertheless, all indications are that Nigerian citizens are strong people. They are risk-takers that are hardworking, intelligent, creative, and industrious. But the quest for quick wealth, fame, vain glory, pride, and evil competition is destroying the land. I go through this lonely agony as l pray the volume will heal the soul of the nation. Nobody wants to go through due process anymore. To them, as long as they can reach the apogee of vain actualization, the means to justify it does not matter. NO! If we want to build a better Nigeria, we must check our attitudes and correctly enforce sanctions on those who have erred.

ATTITUDE TO WORK

If a Nigeria man or woman really want to work, the results will be unbelievable and phenomenal. We are a strong people outfitted with the capabilities and capacity to function anywhere within the human expertise. Needless to say, Nigeria remains one of the most learned population in the United States. This data may surprise you as readers.

So, what has caused us to be known as the poverty capital of the world?

We are versed in science and technology, medical research, nuclear research, IT and communications, structural engineering, and hydrocarbon and seismic capabilities, yet selfishness, greed, and lust for materialism have combined to bring about our reckoning via negative attitude to work.

Many are looking for government jobs because the large bureaucracies permit tenancy, which affects performance in government institutions. We have a lot of ghost workers in the government in Nigeria. This is but just one avenue of building embezzlement in the government.

If we may ask—"Where is our allegiance to our beloved country, Nigeria?"

Where is our obligation or loyalty to our beloved nation?

Americans call America, "Our beloved dream country." The American Dream, a phrase coined by Truslow Adams in his 1931 book *The Epic of America*, is an article of freedom and includes the opportunity for prosperity and success as well as an upward social mobility for the family and children achieved through hard work in a society with few barriers. This teaches us how a legitimate policy can oil the political and economic wheels effortlessly.

In the definition of the American Dream, legal provisions make it better, richer, and barrier-free for everyone in terms of opportunity for each according to his ability or achievement, regardless of social class or circumstances of birth. That is why America is a land of promise and hope.

On the other hand, Nigerians call their beloved country, "A piece of national cake—let me cut my slice." God save us.

I may not be the only Nigerian that read the Abubakar Tafawa Balewa (1957) speech and national anthem. Let us collectively read below an example of his speech together. Maybe we will all learn something from this speech and have a better understanding how citizens should act to build a nation of sterling glory.

> "This has been a great day for Nigeria, and, as the first Prime Minister of the Federation of Nigeria, I am proud to speak to my fellow countrymen tonight. I am proud, and I am humble, too, when I think of the enormous responsibility which has been placed upon me, and my colleagues.

> "... The success of the harvest will depend upon us, and that is why I am glad to speak to you tonight. Every one of us has his part to play in the work of preparing Nigeria for Independence on (2nd of April) October 1st, 1960. I want everyone in Nigeria to realize that this is no easy task, and it cannot be performed by the Federal and Regional Ministers and legislators alone. It is a task for every one of you because it is only by the personal effort of each individual that Independence for the Federation can become a reality in 1960.

> "We have declared our intention of attaining Independence for the Federation on the 2nd of April 1960, and if we wish to take our place among the responsible nations of the world, we must make every effort to see that this aim is achieved, and achieved with an international reputation for good internal government.

> "Nigeria has now reached a critical stage in her history. ... Every Nigerian, whatever his status, and whatever his religion, has his or her share to contribute to this crucial task. I appeal to all my countrymen and women to cooperate with me and my colleagues

to create a better understanding among our peoples, to establish mutual respect, and trust, among all our tribal groups, and to unite in working together for the common cause, the cause for which no sacrifice will be too great.

"I am convinced, and I want you also to be convinced, that the future of this vast country must depend, in the main, on the efforts of ourselves to help ourselves. This we cannot do if we do not work together in unity. Indeed, unity today is our greatest concern, and it is the duty of every one of us to work so that we may strengthen it. This morning I said in the House of Representatives that bitterness due to political differences would carry Nigeria nowhere, and I appealed to the political leaders throughout the country to control their party extremists. To you who are listening tonight I repeat that appeal—Let us put away bitterness and go forward in friendship to Independence.

"... if we are to succeed we must have the loyalty of all Nigerian and expatriate officers in this vital period before self-government is achieved. I should like to reassure all our expatriate staff of our continued Sincerity in the pledges given over the last few years and to promise them that they need have no fears about their future. Their aim and our aim remain what it has always been— the welfare and prosperity of Nigeria. Our political advance will be of no value if it is not supported by economic progress. It is therefore most important that the development plans throughout the country should be carried out with vigour in order that we may have a proper financial standing when, in three years' time, we ask the world to regard us as an independent self-governing nation.

"I would like to remind you of what a great American once said. It was this, 'United we stand, divided we fall'. This statement is as true for Nigeria today as it has been for any other country. The peoples of Nigeria must be united to enable this country to play a full part in shaping the destiny of mankind. On no account should we allow the selfish ambitions of individuals to jeopardize the peace of the thirty-three million law-abiding people of Nigeria. It is the duty of all of us to work for unity and encourage members of all our communities to live together in peace and harmony. The way to do this is to create understanding, mutual respect, and trust. It is important that we should first show respect to each other before asking the world to respect us.

"... but first I would once more tell you how absolutely vital it is for your future and the future Nigeria which your children will inherit that, during this interim period before Independence we should be united. Let us be honest with ourselves, and let us be sincere—we know what we want, and we are sure that we can get it, and get it at the right time, provided we are not delayed by selfish quarrels. At a time like this, we must all turn our minds to Almighty God and seek His guidance and assistance—by His grace, we shall succeed" (Blackpast 2009).

Below is also our Nigerian National Anthem:

Arise, O Compatriots, Nigeria's call obey
To serve our fatherland
With love and strength and faith
The labour of our heroes past
Shall never be in vain
To serve with heart and might
One nation bound in freedom, peace and unity.

Oh God of creation, direct our noble cause
Guide our leaders right
Help our youth the truth to know
In love and honesty to grow
And living just and true

Great lofty heights attain

To build a nation where peace and justice reign

(Nigeria High Commission n.d.)

Similarly, His Excellency President Muhammadu Buhari needs our love, support, and cooperation to build our country to its glory. Without support from all of us, he cannot succeed.

"A single tree cannot make a forest."

Likewise, in 2021, I am appealing to you all to cooperate with our president to make our nation great again.

The labours of our heroes past appear like money down the drain and in vain. We have not maintained anything they laboured for and left for us to continue to build. This is because we are not serving our fathers' land with love and strength and in good faith.

Let us look into our hearts, and after reading Tafawa Balewa's speech and the Nigerian National Anthem, I truly cried seeing Nigeria the way it is today.

If we had followed what he said and abided by our country's anthem, the country would have been better today. We need to take a step back and start over with this doctrine in mind.

My clarion call to our statesmen and the political class who build all those fancy, beautiful mansions is this: do we really have twenty-four-hour electricity in the house? Of course not! I am not talking about the generators that have tremendously raised the hearing threshold hazards for many due to the noise. Who has stifled the nation's quest for a standard power supply? What has happened to the plentiful gas deposits in Nigeria? Who is benefiting from the sleaze?

Yet, generators are what our generations will leave for our children's children.

If they cannot fuel even the generators, they are left alone to live in the darkness as if we are operating in the Dark Ages. What a shameful national calamity.

How can the common man afford to fuel the generators when they are jobless and have been systematically cut off from the big chunks of the cake by the same hegemony that has removed them from the treasure where they wax fat and continue to maintain the status quo? This is a tragedy to be confronted.

The rift is already on the wall.

It is painful to see Nigerians already falling out of love with the nation because of the nonchalant attitudes among us.

Our beloved nation has been dominated by our political and religious leaders that are supposed to be an example for our national conscience. I want to make an emotional appeal to all Nigerians, without exception, to trace the steps back to our forefathers who laid the foundation and who left us a valuable inheritance, believing we will do the same for our children. If they could wake up from their graves to see what their successors have done to their hard labour, they would shed bloody tears as I am doing now.

Our roads and bridges, schools, hospitals, airports, national infrastructure, electricity, transportation, housing, and more have not fared well and are being compared to most third-world countries. Brazil, Malaysia, and most of the Asian Tigers have leaped to industrialized status. Nigeria is still struggling in the take-off stage. That we might become a nation of where all manners of goods must be imported is a direct infliction of an incurable disease observed in our nation.

We need to re-evaluate our priorities. What are our priorities? Our luxurious lifestyles, or our children's futures? Therefore, I implore all Nigerians to think about how these lifestyles marked by greed have underdeveloped us.

Nigeria has been reduced to nothingness and is disrespected in the community of nations. Our dishonour and humiliation in the international community proportionate to the lack of values, inordinate, unruly, and wayward attitudes, and the neglect of what is normative have combined to drag us to our present predicament.

We have come to the crossroads where we need to take a step back, appraise things from the inside out and not from a distance, and see how much this absurdity can be quenched. We need to participate in the growth and development of any noble goal of the government and eschew sitting on the fence.

Together, we can restore our nation as the bride of the black race to its glory.

To the "Giant Africa," once known, we can yet flourish in wealth, healthcare, agriculture, and infrastructure.

Let our actions be congruent with the Nigerian National Anthem.

Let our actions be congruent with the words of Abubakar Tafawa Balewa in his first speech as prime minister.

Let me ask this question, if I may: What are our Nigerians pledging to when they take office? Because I don't get it, if this is what they pledged to!

The National Pledge

I pledge to Nigeria my country
To be faithful, loyal and honest
To serve Nigeria with all my strength
To defend her unity
And uphold her honour and glory
So help me God
(Nigeria High Commission n.d.).

CHAPTER 3

RELIGION AS AN INFLUENTIAL FACTOR IN NIGERIA

Religion is basically a means of man's transcendental union with the super-sensible realms. Man has always known that there is a force invisible to him but yet regulating his sense of right and wrong. Africans' sense of the Almighty was not taught to them by any foreigner. They knew God from various folklore. They associated this with the sky, to an intelligent creator who designed the firmament with no pillars to hold it in place. They saw God in His wondrous ways, delineating night and day, land from seas and oceans, prairies from mountains. The Moon and the Sun, sterling qualities that were inexhaustible, everlasting.

Africans saw God as most majestic, Almighty, omnipotent and omniscient. These characteristics were assigned to Him and regarded so much so that they could not approach Him directly but through lesser gods like our late fore bearers. This was like sacrificing to these demi-gods so their prayers could be taken to God the Father because they felt they were too unholy to stand before His Majesty. Yet, they revered Him.

It was so much in line with the Missionaries and Arab Scholars who descended south and planted Christianity and Islam. The rest is the doctrine of Jesus, also called Christ and Muhammed the Prophet. That African concept of God has never really died and is still practised today.

God is one. Philosophers say reality is one. There are therefore many approaches to reaching the same God. How does this affect national growth or decadence in Nigeria? This is the crux of this chapter.

Religion is one of the most important platforms and has the power to change our society and influence our attitudes toward life and world views at large. This is embedded in its ethics, morality, value system, teachings, charity output, etc.

A religion can play an important role in assisting people to care for and help others. It can contribute as a food basket, a place where people living in poverty can go to seek comfort, food, and shelter for the homeless. What is more, it can provide learning and transmission of cultural and spiritual gifts for people in times of great depression. No wonder Karl Marx asserted that, "Religion is the opiate of the masses" (Papke, David R. 2015).

Religious practices in our society should provide us with worthwhile legacies: a mark to follow. Lessons learned from our religion should encourage us all to do well and promote love, tolerance, and the well-being of individuals, families, and the community.

It is not in vain that while the author was conceptualizing the importance of religion in the national limelight in July 2021, one of the most colourful religious leaders in Nigeria succumbed to the ultimate call. With great humility, we honour you, late Prophet TB JOSHUA of the Synagogue Church of All Nations. With our arms raised in a triumphant salute, you taught and exemplified Christ. What a remarkable and tremendous lesson to learn from you.

You did not live in a mansion, but in an apartment. You visited Bethlehem, the birthplace of our Lord Jesus, and purchased many dialysis machines for kidney treatments in Al-Hussein Hospital in Israel. In 2008, you received an award from the Nigerian government of the Order of the Federal Republic of Nigeria, due to your humanitarian work from the former President of Nigeria. You supplied trailer loads of rice, monies, and relief materials to those who were affected by insurgency in the northern part of Nigeria. Even to the poor communities in the north, you sponsored hundreds of the less privileged. As well, some of whom you sponsored in football are now playing professional football in other countries. You built schools for the less privileged.

With renewed salutation, you were a great man and a good example to be used in this book. This is an example of a true, great religious leader in Nigeria, and even to the ends of the earth you preached the gospel to the lost world.

You had demonstrated in many climates the legacy of ONE LOVE: be it Muslim or Christian. You helped everyone who needed help without any prejudice or tribalism. You were a great, noble man of our generation. We wish this nation was built with the majority of people possessing your character and good heart. You helped people other than your tribe and members of your religion.

In your life, you displayed to everyone that you loved thy neighbour as thyself. That quality was visible to all.

The Gospel of Matthew recorded Jesus's answer: "Love the Lord your God with all your heart and with all your sound and with all your mind. This is the first and greatest commandment. And the second is like it: Love your neighbor as yourself" (Matthew 22:37-39 NIV n.d.).

What an irony! It is so disheartening to see our other Nigerian religious leaders doing just the opposite of the above quotation, who supposedly love their neighbours but also steals from their neighbours or builds fences for separation.

In Nigeria these days, our religious leaders are actually using their platforms to aggregate wealth, preaching faith for success, and living luxurious lifestyles, while inequality among church members is obvious. They build mansions for themselves. They use religious scriptures to their advantages and brainwash people to part with their hard-earned money. Some go about collecting money from the poor who are still struggling and hardly able to feed, clothe, or provide shelter for themselves.

I am a religious person to the core, but this is not right. In addition, some religious leaders are collecting huge sums of donations from people when they know that the money has been stolen from the government public funds, converting the same for personal use.

Despite being aware, they still collect the money and give these dubious persons high, prestigious positions and front-row seats in the church. Anyone would have thought religious leaders would refuse such money, strongly discourage such acts, and preach the truth against it. Is that not what religion is all about—ethics and morality?

Religion is meant to educate and lead us into doing what is right.

That is normative. Everyone would have thought or believed so. But no, it is not. Instead, many of our religious leaders are now competing for wealth. Private jets are what is in vogue for their latest lifestyle.

I watched a video of a Nigerian pastor that visited USA to preach, and during the preaching, stated, "Next time I visit the USA, I am coming on a private jet."

Preaching humanity, love, eternity, morality, honesty, generosity, creativity, and salvation is now secondary. They preach about prosperity and not caring about where or how it is made. Some of our religious leaders are making their congregation contribute to the building of schools, while their poor members cannot afford to send their children to attend those same schools. The fees are extravagantly high, ranging from 500,000 - 3,000,000 naira or above per year, in a country with an average church-member salary of approximately 50,000 naira per month. Abba Father, have mercy.

Only children that come from the high classes can afford the fees. In my own opinion, education ought to be the basic responsibility of government and should be made accessible and affordable for all. Missionary schools should be even more charitable.

This is another touchy phenomenon in our nation.

Some of our religious leaders are using anointing oil, candles, handkerchiefs, etc. as a cover for a miracle, for success, prosperity, and security. Mr. Bill Gates is one of the most successful men in contemporary times, and his wealth was achieved through hard work.

Alhaji Dangote, the richest man in Africa, also worked hard to make his money as a successful businessman. Neither wiped their faces with anointing handkerchiefs before they made their fortunes. Yet, elements of luck come from God. It is 90% hard work first, with luck and prayers following.

Instead of being a good example to our people who look up to them and demonstrating that hard work leads to success, they preach faith to success, they become a negative influence, they are against hard work, and against growth and development for our children who have no deep understanding of how this connects to national growth.

I grew up in Nigeria with a song that goes back to my years in primary school. We sang along with the song in our classes after morning devotion:

"Ise Agbe ni se ilewa
Eni ko sise aa ma jale
Iwe Kiko lai si oko ati ada koyi pe o Koi pe o"

English version:

> "Agriculture is our nation land. Who does not work will end up
> stealing to make a living. Education without an axe and a cutlass
> to cultivate the soil is not enough for you to make a living. It's not
> enough, it's not enough."

All of these messages from our religious leaders are highly contra-
dictory to our upbringing, our pristine culture, and our gospel beliefs. In
my opinion, it is a huge contributing factor to the slow progress in our
nation's developmental stride.

What kind of a message and education are our religious leaders
sending to society, to us, and to our children's children?

The person appointed to a prestigious position of honour is the same
the person sitting in the front-row seat in the church. That same person
is the reason our roads are bad, why our children sit in darkness at night
to do their homework because there is no constant power. That same
person is the reason why our children attend school without a chair or
table to write on. They are the reason why your brother or sister had
that fatal accident, lost their life because of the dilapidated roads or big
potholes on our highways. Is anyone with me? No doubt, it will have an
impact on ourselves and on our children, as we are already seeing in our
nation.

It seems many Nigerians want to be pastors, even if they have no
calling. Every street in Nigeria is littered with churches. In addition,
almost all of our children seem to want to be a politician so they can have
huge sums of money to donate at public functions, so they can have the
dubious prestige and social position and be treated with special dignity
and recognition. What a colossal shame.

While many people in our nation have a mindset for and aspire
to being a religious leader with the greed for huge sums of financial
earnings, this is not supposed to be how it is; it should be a calling. On

the other hand, our nation is suffering due to the lack of other diverse jobs and professional callings that would have enhanced the nation to grow and evolve into a developed nation, yet the urge is for quick wealth through these channels. It is amazing.

Furthermore, attendance at our religious services is not directly linked to a stable family life, well-behaved children, and strong family values—because of its moral decadence, teachings that was supposed to reduce crime, drug abuse, hatred, selfishness, self-centredness in our society. It could also have promoted patriotism amongst the citizens.

However, there seems to be a decline, an atrophy of religious adherence to its teachings and doctrines, that has led to societal declension and retrogression. Politics, greed, selfishness, pride, and lust for materialism has entered our religious houses. Today, we only recognize the rich, the well-to-do, and the privileged ones, while we ignore and look upon with disdain the poor, the downtrodden, and those who really need our love, care, and support. We have turned our religious houses into commercial centres, places for personal gains, and avenues to enrich ourselves. Are we different from those we see and label as thieves or corrupt government entities in our society?

Religious teachings taught us to love, forgive, and tolerate. They taught us to be our brother's keeper and how to be a good citizen. They teach us moral standards.

But greed, selfishness, and lustfulness have made us abandon the good teachings we received from our religious books, which is supposed to be the bedrock for a better society and a society free of immoralities.

Our religious houses are supposed to be a light, a place of refuge for the rejected, a place of strength for the weak, the eyes for the blind, and a place where those who mourn can be comforted. But we have diverted and polluted the true doctrines and morality handed to us by true, old-time religion. They have concerted today's religious platforms into personal gains, building imposing empires for themselves and building schools that a poor man cannot afford. This is not unto our God. Until we renounce these perversions and repent for these negative attitudes, there will be continued immorality in our society.

The majority of us have our roots connected to one religion or another; even those in affairs of national rulership, we hear teachings of love, peace, co-existence, discipline, and orderliness. We hear sermons to be our brother's keepers, to live in unity, but most often we allow personal interest and selfishness to divide us and ensnare us in enmity to one to another. A lot of our religious teachers are not helping our society to be better. Some teachings received from them emanate from selfish ambitions, lustful desires, and the quest for material filch and specula-tion. Some incorrect teachings have caused a deviation and a divergence from the original teachings, values, and administrations passed on to us by our religious books.

As religious teachers, in order for us to have a society filled with love, we must preach unity, love, tolerance, co-existence, patriotism, and moral disciplines.

RELIGIOUS INTOLERANCE

Religious intolerance is defined by the refusal to accept or tolerate the faith and belief system of another person. Religious intolerance is rooted in strong religious affinity. In Nigeria, it has caused a lot of religious bloodletting, division, and hatred amongst our people.

As citizens, we must consider humanity before religion. Religion may divide us because of beliefs, hence the potential to divide the nation and retard growth. However, humanity should unite us together. As humans, we have the right to practice whatever religion we have chosen, as long as it doesn't affect or trample on the rights of others or affect our national cohesion. God Almighty values humanity more than religion;

it is wrong to force another person to imbibe your own religion and its beliefs, and it's wrong to put down another religion as less important. God gave us liberty to choose, not offend anyone. All religions matter in importance and deserve all our respect.

Condemning another religion is a violation of other people's rights and hence an injustice to the people involved.

Although the focus seems to be mostly on the Christian faith, we have three major religious groups in Nigeria: Christians, Muslims, and Traditionalists.

We know the crises the Islamic religious sect have caused in Nigeria, such as insurgency in the Northeast, religious violence in Jos, Plateau State, Southern Kaduna of Zango Kataf and the Maitasine violence in the northern part of Nigeria, killing and forcing many Christians in the north to denounce their Christ and accept Islam. In Nigeria, we have two courts in one country: federal court and Islamic Sharia court. It is like having two constitutions with one flag.

The issue of selfishness can be seen in every other religion, as well as in both Islamic and the traditional leaders.

As Matin Luther King Jr. stated, "Injustice anywhere is a threat to justice everywhere" (KeepInspiring.me. n.d.).

This religious intolerance has led to so much pain, relative deprivation, segregation, violence toward one another, unhealed hatred, rancour, and bitter divisions because of supremacy rights.

Religious intolerance has crept into our politics and our economic and national life. Imagine a society where getting a job, political appointment, or promotion is not based on merit but on religious considerations. How will such a nation grow or develop economically? If getting help is linked to your faith or religious background, how will such a country have vibrant economic growth? Our existence must be about humanity and not our religious beliefs. We have to learn to accommodate, love, and help one another irrespective of our religion. Humanity must come first.

In a local government in one of the states in Nigeria, during an election, one of the aspirants of that local government chairmanship election, an obvious contestant, came with some political thugs to where the voting was going on peacefully and threatened everyone, insisting that the locality consists of many people of his own religious group who belong to his religious faith, and that anyone who votes for another person from any other religion will be dealt with or killed.

Oh, I wept. I was not even allowed to ask my question. Where is our humanity? We are better united than divided; we will do more in unity than in division.

As a nation, we have to learn to tolerate each other regardless of the religion we belong to. Remember—we were humans first before religious persons. Let's put humanity first. Let's guide our words and actions toward one another, let us love each other and live together as human irrespective of our faith and belief differences.

DANGERS OF FALSE RELIGIOUS TEACHINGS

In our families, communities, and even in the nations of the world, false teachings from our religious teachers have caused much harm and conflict. It has triggered religious heresies and extremism backed by overzealousness amongst the followers. This has led many into errors, murderous wars, and ethnic cleansing. Some of these teachings are resultant effects of greed for supremacy and superiority of a dominant religion.

Some religious leaders teach their followers to criticize, hate, and misinterpret other religion in order to gain supremacy, not knowing that the ignorance of their followers would bring about a religious war of a dimension not foreseen. Instead of teaching our followers co-exis-tence, love, peace, unity, and humanity, we are teaching a superiority complex—whose God is real or not. Yet, the true God is the only one. Some religious leaders teach their followers that anyone who is not of their faith should not be associated with it. No! It ought not to be so. Incorrect teaching has destroyed the fabric of our co-existence and our common goal, which is to build a nation where peace and justice may reign supreme. We long for a society where we can put our religious dif-ferences aside and live peacefully together to build a better future for ourselves and our children yet to come.

According to Martin Luther King Jr., "Nothing in the world is more dangerous than sincere ignorance and conscientious stupidity" (KeepInspiring.me n.d.).

Religious leaders must be careful of what they teach their followers. Incorrect teachings can destabilize and unsettle our communities and destroy our purpose for existence. Let love lead.

Just like Martin Luther King Jr. said, "I have decided to stick with love" (KeepInspiring.me n.d.). Similarly, I have too.

As a result of my loving, caring heart for my people and for our nation, and despite Canada being my place of residence, I own a charitable or-ganization called Early Interventions Health Foundation that has been registered in Nigeria since 2015 that some of our Nigerians at home have benefited from. To date, I have spent at least $40,000 helping with early interventions in health care services. It is a mission of love. It is my passion to see my people free from malaria, high blood pressure, cardiac complications, typhoid, visual acuity checks, and many quick health care interventions and advocacies.

Lack of true love amongst ourselves and being our brother's hater is too great a burden to bear. Hatred is destroying our nation and retarding our developmental growth. Hatred, tribalism, greediness, and selfishness have not permitted us to cooperate collectively in ONE LOVE to support our leaders at all levels of authority to build our nation and restore the glory to the "Giant's Africa."

Remember, Nigeria will not build itself. We, the people in it, will build it. Yoruba oo, Hausa oo, Igbos oo, Muslims oo, Christians oo, or other religious groups and nationalities—we are all Nigerians.

Whatever we do to the country, we do for ourselves. If we recklessly build it, it is reckless depression for all of us, including you and me. If we build it happily, it will be happiness for all of us.

What about you?

What have you done either as an individual or a religious organization? What are you doing as your contribution to build our nation? I want you to ask yourself those questions. Consider what you can do to help our nation.

This is what our nation needed yesterday and still needs right now. Tomorrow might be too late. Nigeria needs us all—no excuses or exceptions. We must collectively start the new journey today. God bless Nigeria.

CHAPTER 4

OVER-CENTRALIZATION OF POWER

How does this concept relate to our consideration of the collective contribution to the moral and ethical decadence in present-day Nigeria? How, what, and when did power, which is a repository of the people, flee to the centre? How is this power used in the annexation of people's rights and subjugation of everything morally right in our society? What visible consequences could be seen from the reaction of the citizenry and their provoked jealousies that cause monumental unethical and immoral behaviour in our society?

To provide an understanding of the above, we will consider in brief the historical nature of the nation states that became Nigeria at Amalgamation in 1914. We will consider:

1. Pre-colonial nation states in Nigeria

2. Post Independent Nigeria and power relations

3. Contemporary political power relations in Nigeria

But before then, here is my take on the use of power from the centre. If we are not ready to sacrifice something, we are not ready to serve the people. What are these sacrifices? It is important for us Nigerians to ask ourselves some serious questions. What is the most important thing to a Nigerian? What kind of factors from our childhood make us desperate and dangerously competitive? Sometimes we are under pressure from our parents and peers to "prove ourselves."

Could a power achieve all that it wished, it would strive for absolute security. But absolute security for one power means an absolute insecurity for all others, hence it is never part of a "legitimate" settlement and can only be achieved through conquest.

If national and international order could be constructed with the clarity of a mathematical axiom, powers would consider themselves factors in a balance and arrange their adjustments to achieve a perfect equilibrium between the forces of aggression and the forces of resistance. But an exact balance is impossible, and not only because of the difficulty of predicting the aggressor; it is chimerical. Above all, because while states or sub-national groups may appear to outsiders as factors in a security arrangement, they appear domestically as expressions of a historical existence. No state or group will submit to a settlement, however well balanced and however "secure," which seems to deny its vision of itself.

Therefore, there exists two kinds of equilibrium: a general equilibrium that makes it risky for one power or group of powers to attempt to impose its will on the remainder, and a particular equilibrium that defines the historical relations of certain powers among each other. The former is a deterrent against a general violence; the latter the condition for a smooth cooperation. An international or national order is therefore rarely born out of the consciousness of harmony. For even when there is an agreement about legitimacy and approach, the concepts of the requirements of security (freedom) will vary according to the geographical position and the history of each contending power or group.

To come to grips with the issues of these cases, therefore, is to begin the endlessly fascinating study of world politics by understanding what drives men, groups, and nations. But sadly—indeed tragically—the timeliness of this book needs no emphasis. As conflicts lead to tension, and tension into violent expressions, innocent people are deliberately killed, maimed, and arrested. The headlines of the news bulletins become all too sickeningly familiar, and the feeling of impotent fury that overcomes us after each outrage gradually gets numbed by violent repetition.

This book is a direct, candid response to the impact of events in Nigeria, and it examines vividly the ideological and the genealogy of moral bankruptcy in Nigeria. It discusses the motivation and tactical thinking of such men, groups, and governments involved in such shameful behaviours. In all, it presents to the reader a deeply disturbing analysis of a vital phenomenon that all of us are now forced to live with. Tony Burton (1975) points out that "One can only cure a sick man by understanding the nature of his complaint.

Therefore, this work is aimed at understanding these complaints so that solutions and control can be sought in the spirit of justice, equity, and respect for the rights of individuals, or that some sort of political balance, like the Congress of Vienna in the autumn of 1814 which lasted for almost a century, is obtained.

It seems like a simple and well thought-out volume that never caters to anybody's lust for moral decadence. To some it may be upsetting, but above all, it is sensible and provocative. In each case, the interaction of men, ideologies, sub-national interests, and the dynamic forces has been set out. It invites debate, engagement, and thought in its examination of both the structural and manifested behaviours by subsuming and treating them as exogenous variables to the phenomenon of ethical and moral bankruptcy in our land.

Perhaps some will find us guilty of an eclecticism gone wild, but we cannot but feel that writers as disparate as Ted Robert Gurr, Frantz

Fanon, Ahn Chung-Si, Douglas Hibbs, Bowles et al. have each made a fundamental contribution to the understanding of the problem of political violence derived from ethical and moral decadence.

Man's nature seems to permit disobedience. From creation, he rebelled. He chose to err. God did not take away his willpower. But we need to understand how his motivation and cognition affect the level of his deviance. It may be perhaps because man is a political animal.

Men seemed to have pinned their hopes and fears on the idea that somehow the social, economic, and political problems that face any nation can be resolved through domination. When such ideals as freedom, justice, and equality are at stake, it is not surprising to find people reacting strongly and somewhat less than dispassionately. The strong emotional impact of even a minor protest indicates quite clearly that when total political upheaval is at stake, only few people can remain neutral. Yet, an analysis of this is not so easy for it must incorporate highly complex events and an understanding of numerous related phenomena.

Does moral and ethical bankruptcy include apathy and corruption as key characteristics? Are these shameful acts an effective tool for accelerating social reforms? Are their use ever justified to achieve either of the objectives of our commonality? Are there always better alternatives available? Are the use of immoral and unethical behaviours in relation to social change a phenomenon unique to our nation alone? If not, what lessons, if any, are contained in our national experience? It would be tempting to try to provide an easy answer to the complex political, moral, religious, economic, and social questions raised by the issues of moral decadence. In fact, this work may not provide sufficient answers, but may raise many additional questions.

Nigeria turned into an epic disaster, causing an equally monumental despair in all of Africa and the international community. Ours had been the dilemma of a juggler—a tearful separation of the soul of the nation.

Over the years, many lives have been lost due to such criminal behaviour. Many public and private investments have been destroyed. There has been political instability, injustices, strikes, riots, protests, and demonstrations—a terrible precedent. Spinning off from the above, our education system has been badly defaced, our economy strangled. Democracy has been raped—slapped in broad daylight. Social life has lost its opulence. Life has become hopeless. Hardship is conspicuous on the faces of Nigerians. Nigeria and Nigerians lost their pride, flamboyance, and integrity in high places. Political governance assumed a new dimension. Government could no longer govern by display, example, or persuasion, but by sheer force.

If all of these occurred where there are no welfare programs for the poor, sick, young, the aged, the invalid, the under-employed, and unemployed, then there are obviously political, social, and economic dislocations in the country, all arising from our collective, unpatriotic behaviours. This is what has triggered violent riots in Argentina, Algeria, Venezuela, Sudan, Lebanon, and Jordan, to mention but a few.

POWER RELATIONS IN PRE-COLONIAL NATION STATES OF NIGERIA

Before the arrival of the British, the Nigerian people, as we are known today, were isolated, autonomous nations of people engaged at contact points in trade of all sorts and in occasional warfare. Evidence of this early contact abounds in the oral histories of many Nigerian ethnic groups. These peoples were grouped in communities that ranged from empires to village communes, each fending for themselves to the best of their abilities. Most of the empires were found in the north, such as the Kanem-Borno Empire, as well as powerful emirates and caliphate. To the southwest, the people were organized into fiercely independent kingdoms, and to the southeast, the concept and culture of para-democratic tendencies, almost bordering on anarchy, made it impossible for the emergence of kingdom or empire (Arthur Nwankwo 1984).

An early external influence on the northern people of Nigeria that changed the course of our history was Islam. Islam filtered into what is now known as Nigeria from North Africa. It introduced a new way of life, a new religion, an educated, governing elite, and finally, a forced unity amongst its northern adherents. Through Jihad and trade, Islam attempted to spread toward the southern part of the country and made great strides before it was stopped by the British in 1874.

The British, who had by then abolished the slave trade, replaced slavery with what they called legitimate commerce—that is, a one-sided trade in tropical produce. At the same time as the British stopped both Islamic expansionism and the slave trade, they launched a program to make Nigerians Christians, promoting missionary activity particularly in the southern part of the country.

The natural result of the conquest was colonization, and the British, backed by gunboats, accomplished these feats in Nigeria with phenomenal rapidity and legitimized their exclusive monopoly of commerce and territory by mid-century, first in the Bights of Benin and Biafra (now Bonny), and then in Lagos in 1861.

Through the initiative of the United African Company (UAC), a consortium of British businesses formed in 1876, most of northern Nigeria was preserved as a British sphere of influence.

Consequent upon this, therefore, at the Berlin Conference in 1884, the continent was divided up among the imperial powers. Most of what is Nigeria today was awarded to Great Britain, and in 1885, the UAC received a royal charter to administer the territory on behalf of Imperial Britain. This charter was revoked in 1899, and the British government began to administer the territory directly.

Britain colonized Nigeria piecemeal; first, they gathered together the northern sectors into a single administrative unit and called it the protectorate of Northern Nigeria. Then, they combined the Niger Coast protectorate and Lagos Colony in 1906 and called it the protectorate of Southern Nigeria.

Finally, in 1914, the Northern and Southern protectorates were amalgamated under Lord Fredrick Luggard who became the first Governor-General of Nigeria, and so began the political history of modern Nigeria that went through the grudging constitutional and nationalist agitation until Nigeria achieved independence on October 1, 1960 (Nwankwo 1984).

POST INDEPENDENT NIGERIA AND POWER RELATIONS.

At independence, Nigeria was organized into three regions: the Northern, Western and Eastern regions, each with a Premier who governed the region. There was the Federal Prime Minister and the Governor-General at the centre. This was the British model of Parliament with a bicameral legislature. Each region or confederate was responsible for its development except for national currency and armed forces—each made a decision for its people through their elected representatives. Power was never usurped by the centre of government.

The major problem with every emerging independent country in Africa was the rapid decolonization, resulting in the disparity between the high aspirations of the people and the capacity of the new government to implement good and fair policies (Samuel Ayough 1976).

When a society is out of joint socially and politically, says Samuel Huttington, there is bound to be disequilibrium. What follows is a cataclysm either in the form of a revolution or protests and demonstrations, or where there is a political army, a military intervention. The latter is precisely what happened in Nigeria on January 15, 1966, when a group of soldiers staged the first coup d'état in Nigeria.

Prior to that time, the country had been on a trajectory course of self-destruction. Since 1960, political brinkmanship, tribalism, nepotism, and regionalism were the order of the day. The Action Group crisis, which first started as a leadership tussle between the party and leader Obafemi Awolowo and his deputy, Samuel Akintola, soon burst into the open, degenerated into a clash of personalities, and eventually split the party lines into two warring factions. The result was the bloody, violent riot in the Western House of Assembly in 1962 and the ultimate declaration of a state of emergency in the whole region by then Prime Minister Abubakar Tafewa Balewa.

But that was one of the many preludes to the major disaster. The 1963 census controversy was another. The controversial figures were rejected mostly by politicians from the southern part of the country. The 1964 federal elections did not help matters either. Accusations and counter ac-cusations of rigging polluted the air. For some time, there was a political stalemate as the President, Dr. Nnamdi Azikiwe, hesitated to invite the leader of the Nigerian National Alliance (NNA), to form a cabinet.

The following year, 1965, was a year of gloom as political and social unrest descended on the Nigerian landscape. The Tiv riots in Benue Province further charged the atmosphere and put into question the state of security in the country. The last straw was the October 1965 election in the west. Democracy was in disarray because the election was manipu-lated in favour of the Nigerian National Democratic Party (NNDP), the ruling party of Akintola. This election brought more violence than before as the "Wild West" bounced back like a rubber ball in a wanton display of violence, anger, and vengeance. Arson, murder, mayhem, and looting took over. By December, there had been a total breakdown of law and order in Western Nigeria. Operation Wetie, in which houses, property, and persons of opponents were doused in petrol and set ablaze, reduced houses and motor vehicles into ashes and turned political opponents into human torches.

The Balewa government did nothing to stem the tidal waves of unrest. Life became more and more unsafe as each day passed by. Instead of declaring a state of emergency as he did in 1962 during the Action Group crisis, Balewa chose to sit on the fence. He played the Nigerian Nero, fiddling with the Commonwealth Prime Minister's Conference in Lagos on the future of Zimbabwe while his own country burned.

The prime minister thus became the proverbial foolish man who put fire in his own house and went to sleep. Somebody else had to carry out a rescue mission to save both the house and the household from destruction.

The army played that role in the wee hours of January 15, 1966, when the Majors, led by Kaduna Nzeogwu, struck.

The coup appeared noble and faultless in concept but questionable in execution. It was supposed to be carried out simultaneously in Kaduna, Lagos and Enugu, and Benin and Ibadan—all regional cities. Lagos and Kaduna saw fire, and Benin and Enugu saw little or no action.

In Kaduna, Operation Damisa, as the coup was code named, was a huge success under the direct command of Nzeogwu. The premier's lodge was stormed and the premier, who had hidden in a heap of his wives, was killed in the encounter. In Ibadan, the main target fell into the soldiers' dragnet. Deputy Premier Fani Kayode surrendered and was promptly arrested. Akintola was killed in an exchange of fire with soldiers at the Government House.

In Lagos, something went wrong. The main target, General Ironsi, miraculously escaped arrest and professionally recovered in time to organize a counter move. Thus, while the Kaduna operation was carried out with surgical precision, the Lagos putsch failed. The political coup seems to have been a blessing. There was a spontaneous outburst of rejoicing all over the country with popular demonstrations of support for the military takeover. The first full impact was the immediate calm restored in the burning west.

In the north, reaction was cautious. The initial joy evaporated with the realization that the northern political leaders and senior army officers had an unfair share of the casualty figures, while power, which the north had controlled at the federal level since independence, was suddenly discovered to have slipped away. The planners had apparently staged the coup to establish a new social and political order. According to them, it was an attempt to get rid of corruption, tribalism, and nepotism. Nzeogwu, in his major broadcast over Radio Kaduna, said:

> "Our enemies are the political profiteers, swindlers, the men in the high and low places who seek bribes, and demand 10%, those that seek to keep the country divided permanently so that they can remain in office as Minister and VIPs of waste, the tribalists and the nepotists..."

The feeling among the northern elites, then, was that the coup was an Igbo plot to take over the country. General Ironsi, the new strongman, did nothing to allay their fears. Instead, he came up with Decree No.14 of May 24, 1966, abolishing the federal setup and creating a unitary state. That is how POWER moved to the centre in Nigeria.

Violent protests and demonstrations in the north greeted this political move. Furthermore, Ironsi's failure to bring to justice the arrested coup plotters only helped to aggravate the seething anger of northerners over the way the January coup was carried out.

Thus, in the early hours of July 29, 1966, Major T.Y. Danjuma and a group of junior army officers and other ranks surrounded Government House, Agodi, and Ibadan. Their mission, according to Danjuma, was to arrest the head of the Federal Military Government and Supreme

Commander of the Armed Forces, Major General J.T.U. Aguiyi Ironsi, who was in Ibadan for a conference. The second instance of political violence, sometimes referred to as a counter coup, had begun. Ironsi and his host, the military governor of the western group of provinces, Lieutenant Colonel Adekunle Fajuyi, were arrested and killed, and Ironsi's government collapsed.

Eventually, Lieutenant Colonel Gowon, Chief of Army Staff emerged as the new leader, and he assumed office on August 1, 1966.

Gowon ruled Nigeria for nine long years, maintaining the power at the centre and creating twelve states. There were chains of rapid, violent events, such as the pogroms in the north, which boiled down to civil war.

On July 29, 1975, General Murtala Mohammed staged in a coup. In February 1976, seven new states were approved and created by the Military junta who kept power at the centre.

On February 13, 1976, a group of soldiers led by Lieutenant Colonel Dimka, taking advantage of the lax security profile of his government, waylaid Murtala on his way to work and brutally murdered him. The coup, however, did not succeed. General O.M.A. Obasanjo took over. He called off power from the centre with his Military Junta, and on October 1, 1979, handed over power to a civilian government under Shehu Shagari, the leader of the National Party of Nigeria.

Nigerians had achieved their desire of civilian government, but this was to hasten rather than halt the slippage of the economy. This administration ostensibly did not fly. The rate at which the country lost foreign exchange through fictitious imports became alarming. Corruption had been glorified.

Businessmen, companies, and government agents were using import licences to buy goods that were of little to no relevance to the country's development and for which those licences was not issued. Worst of all, imports became the easiest way for foreign companies and their domestic agents to transfer billions of naira to their countries. Shagari also manipulated the elections and secured his second tenure in office.

Nigerians did not keep quiet. Inflation was hitting hard too. Shagari, instead of berthing the ship to shore, left it to float and drift in high seas, thus when Nigerians heard the voice of Sani Abacha early in the morning of December 31, 1983, informing them that the government of Shehu Shagari had been overthrown, many heaved a sigh of relief that the end had come to that seemingly bankrupt regime.

General Buhari and Tunde Idiagbon took over and tried to sanitize things. By this time, power was solidly determined from the centre. Yet less than twenty months later, on August 27, 1985, Nigerians were again awakened by the voice of another, Brigadier Joshua Dogonyaro, who told them amid the sad sound of martial music, that the military had no choice but to remove the Buhari regime, which somehow managed to squander the unprecedented goodwill it enjoyed when it came to power. Babangida thus replaced him.

General Ibrahim Babangida ruled as a tyrant for eight long years and systematized corruption and accentuated the destruction of the moral and ethical foundation we are decrying today.

Over-centralization of power moved on the crescendo as well as all the evil machinations we see today in officialdom. Babangida sought to cling to power and bully the whole nation into silence and submission. This was a murderous claim to office that Nigerians did not allow. Hence, on the 27th of August 1993, he was ignominiously compelled to step aside after he annulled a mostly free and fair election that was clearly won by Alhaji M.K.O. Abiola of the Social Democratic Party.

An interim national government headed by Chief Ernest Shonekan took over, but power was flowing from somewhere else. This was challenged by vocal Nigerians who left power on the street for many months of violent protests until Abacha took it. He destroyed all the political structures and usurped power, claiming, "Enough is enough." He also ruled for eight years, and Nigeria was ostracized from the international community because of his tyrannical use of state power. Sadly, and indeed tragically, he died in June 1998 and General Abdulsalami Abubakar took over.

He tried to steer the ship of national unity, but power was not significantly shared with the people. To calm the mood of the nation after the death of Abiola in detention, Obasanjo emerged as the new civilian president after the elections. Nigerians had witnessed the third republic with power concentrated at the centre.

CONTEMPORARY OVER-CENTRALIZATION OF POWER IN NIGERIA.

The Obasanjo second coming as the civilian president was thought to have stabilized the polity and give the nation a new direction. But corruption was unabated because everyone saw the centre as the fulcrum of having a share of the national wealth. Of the three arms of government, the judiciary and federal legislature were effectively controlled by the executive. Whatever bill or policies that were made must receive the approval and consent of the president. The state governors turned themselves into private potentates. The autonomy of the third tier of government, the local government, was technically neutralized, and their financial independence subsumed in the state government. With the collapse of the local government administration, all eyes were directed at the centre where corruption has been the defining ethos of our people.

Grassroots roles were abandoned. Agriculture from rural areas suffered. People wanted a taste of what politics could offer. It was no longer service to the nation but personal interest of family and friends.

This continued in the Goodluck Ebele Johnathan regime as political parties fought each other and used government funds to run political campaigns. Discontent and moral bankruptcy had been attained the highest level, and a time bomb was already in place.

With President Buhari's second coming, the trend had not been redressed. Over-centralization of power in the centre was the reason why there was an accentuated demand for restructuring, fiscal federalism, a new, people-oriented constitution, and the freedom for the regions to go separate ways if equality, equity, and fairness was not available in a country of over 250 languages of ethnic nationalities.

If national wealth is the exclusive right of the ruling elites from a particular section of the country; if appointments into federal positions is the exclusive preserve of the northern hegemony; if ownership of the oil wells and licences are cornered by others using political power against the pauperization of the tribal people; if herdsmen would kill, maim, and rape women and children of other tribes and destroy daily their farmlands and their means of survival; if senate and federal House of Representatives could pass an unpopular bill by means of northern automatic majority in parliament against electronic transmission of election results; and if 3% of the Petroleum Industry Bill is approved for the owners of the oil wealth from whose proceeds 90% has been used to develop other places for a period exceeding fifty years without com-mensurate considerations of the ecological despoliation of the tribal homelands against the demanded 5%, while 30% is proposed for regions where exploration have not yet taken place, then there is an urgent need for power devolution by which the Nigerian people would constructively participate in decisions affecting their daily lives.

The ethical and moral decadence experienced in the Nigerian social space is nothing but the direct impact of poor leadership and brinkman-ship. Banditry, arson, kidnapping, cultism, armed robbery, Bokoharam, political thuggery, and prostitution are all manifestations of the poverty our political elites have foisted onto the nation through corrupt practices.

However, this paper is a collective acceptance of the fact that we all have erred, and so we must come down to the place where the primacy of reason must reign.

Our leaders know the seeming mood of frustration in the nation right now, for it is the nation's present mood and our collective amnesia that interest groups and governments try to impress upon the Nigerian people that the nightmares they brought upon the nation was/is, in fact, a blessing. But we would be foolish to allow ourselves to become totally ignorant. Only irresponsible people can place their hope on some sort of help from abroad. No handouts will solve our national problems. Our destiny is squarely in our own hands. It appears that our constant readiness to forget allows sinners to don the cloak of saints every time Nigeria faces a crisis. Some of those who sought to defend truth and life in the manner they know best were regarded as traitors and enemies of the state. The truth has been forced to stand on its head.

These are sad and tragic times for a nation that is mature at sixty-one years of age but is still having the elementary problem of searching for its political soul and stability. This is a moment of yet another turn in our cyclic crisis. But let us not, because of today, forget yesterday, just because our leaders want to canonize themselves and the interests they represent. They, too, made their contributions to the cumulative tragedy that is today's inheritance. Today's wound is open and fresh, but yesterday's scars remain. Yesterday's men, women, groups, and governments who inflicted the scars must be constantly reminded that the victims have not been forgotten.

Goffman (1975) noted that if we abandon the role allotted to us by society, we run a great risk—either of losing face or of losing our freedom. He might have well added that we may also lose our lives.

Indeed, a trend in sociology has been to try to define, in particular, the social significance of the right to die not just at any time, cause, or place, but to reveal the inequality that still exists in this respect. "How can there be equality in death when there is so little in life?" There is the objection raised by sociologists who fear glorification of structural violence like corruption for its own sake and decry the attraction it exerts on certain thinkers of the "left" today. Hannah Arendt (1972), for instance, attempts to demystify the crimes advocated by the "new left" and fears that, "Purifying violence sanctioned as an end in itself does not constitute a valid answer to the social debate." She does, however, admit that, "In certain circumstances, violence is the only way to balance the scales." But what, exactly, are those circumstances?

Governmental rigidity, marginalization, systemic exploitation, religious intolerance, domination and oppression of others, injustice, and inequalities are not God-given. Biology is immutable, and no item of inequality is carried in the genes. We are first biological beings before we are social beings. Therefore, all these factors of moral bankruptcy are mere vitiating and trivializing behaviours in our society and can be addressed.

Thus, the conscience of our nation seems to be confused to the point of schizophrenia, and the inevitable disappointments, frustrations, and illogicalities of our political instability are wrongly interpreted as nothing but the fruits of evolving democratic culture and blunders. How can our nation advance in a condition of anarchy, distrust, illegal leadership, lawlessness, riots, dissatisfaction, suspicion, and, most of all, a clique of highly sensitized elitism... that they alone must rule, or Heaven falls? How can we wrap our deep patriotism in the cloak of a seemingly nonchalant equanimity?

When the dominant group insists on political domination against the "weak," not on grounds of expediency but as a moral "right," it is not only raising the issue to a more elevated plane, but is indeed posing a dilemma that might provoke rounds of violence. For a "right" is established by acquiescence, not by a claim, and a claim not generally accepted is merely the expression of an arbitrary will. Moreover, it is the moral claim that it cannot be compromised, precisely because it justifies itself by consideration beyond expediency. Therefore, the Heavens will not fall.

Nothing that is worth doing can be achieved in our lifetime alone; therefore, we are saved by hope. Nothing which is true or fair makes complete sense in any immediate context of history; therefore, we must be saved by faith. Nothing we do, however virtuous, can be accomplished alone, and therefore we should be saved by cooperation. No virtuous act is quite as virtuous from the standpoint of our political friend or foe as it is from our standpoint; therefore, we must be saved by the final form of peace, which is tolerance. Thus, with tolerance, we try too simply to make sense out of life, striving for harmonies between men and nature, men and groups in society, and men and their ultimate destinies.

When all is said and done, and there is love, good faith, good intention, equality and equal access to resources and decision making with malice toward none, with love for all, with firmness in the right, with emphasis on what ought to be and not what was nor what is, let us with God, Allah, or Creator in mind bind up the wound of the past between the oppressor and the oppressed, between the weak and the strong, between the dominant and the dominated. For whenever judgment defines the limits of human striving, it creates the possibility of a humble acceptance of those limits. Within those limits, peace and stability find a lodging place. With trust and a dependable attitude, they form a network of roles which have a strong influence on one another for overall development and national stability. This calls for collaboration, coordination, and integration.

CHAPTER 5

MISMANAGEMENT OF PUBLIC FUNDS

Most Nigerians seems to be lackadaisical even when serious national issues are brought forward. This appears to have stemmed from the lack of morality amongst our citizenry. In the words of Martin Luther King Jr., "Every man must decide whether he will walk in the light of creative altruism or in the darkness of destructive selfishness" (KeepInspiring.me n.d.). This appears to hold true of the Nigerian situation, but until we start being honest with ourselves and face the realities our country, we will not experience the desired changes we are seeking.

One of the main factors that have contributed to the decadence in our nation is corruption in officialdom. Nigeria's lack of citizenship integrity could best explain this. Often, you will see many Nigerians mortgaging their rights because of a plate of rice, a loaf of bread, a bowl of beans, a gallon of vegetable oil, T-shirts, umbrellas for market people, a packet of salts, or a paltry five thousand naira, etc. In addition, the only time you will ever see our politicians at the grassroots is during elections. After that, they are gone to the cities and squander public funds in hotel accommodations and never return to their communities until another election. Isn't this true, people?

Nigerians do not know how to protect their rights. Political leaders go to constituencies to buy the rights and the voices of the people with little tokens, and many Nigerians simply fall for that—poverty might also be a contributing factor. It is similar to selling our birthright. Why? This is because we are looking for immediate satisfaction. What about tomorrow? When you give some of our people the equivalent of a dollar, they can go the extra mile to destroy one another, even burning down their houses out of poverty or for such trivial reasons as greed and lack of goodwill to one another. Until we change from this immediate gratification syndrome we have developed over the years, we will end up nowhere, as we are already seeing.

Until we stop trading our rights and conscience for a loaf of bread and immediate gratification and put the interest of our national development in focus, the interest of our children's children and our own welfare and concerns will keep repeating the same story.

As Nigerians, we need to understand that the beauty and growth we all crave will come only if we put our immediate gratification aside and collectively fight for our national development. When we give some of our people just five thousand naira, they can go destroy government property. They may even go to the extreme of taking somebody's life because of money. We need to change from these destructive and criminal acts and start taking responsibility for our actions that contribute to the failure of our national growth.

Some time ago, I was in Nigeria during an election. I was at the polling unit trying to exercise my franchise. A certain politician had obviously sent his boys with some money to bribe the voters into voting against their preferred candidate, urging them to vote for him. In order to take home a token, some voters shamelessly and openly broke ranks and went with these boys and returned to vote against their conscience. These same Nigerians who voted against their conscience knew the candidate they voted for did not have the moral criteria, character, or integrity of a worthy leader. Many across the nation still vote in like manners for the same self-obsession. REWARD MENTALITY—what I can get, irrespective of who I vote for.

We need to come to our senses: look around our community, and look at the person you voted for yesterday. Today, their children have all gone out of the country to school abroad. They built the best mansions on your street, acquired about five properties for rental and income generation, and have six to ten cars parked at their house. Yet, your bribe of five thousand naira is long gone. He still has more money to buy your conscience again, so he may keep subjugating you. Can we not all see how the vicious circle repeats itself? Tomorrow, due to the same token again, we will vote for this person again and again. Where are your own children? Of course, they are in a school that has no roof over them, no chairs, no books, no qualified teachers, etc.

At the cost of our conscience, the person you voted for yesterday is now living an extravagant, luxurious lifestyle. He classified you and denigrated you in your own community as a second-class citizen. Am I the only one seeing this?

How much is our parliamentarians' salary per year?

So where are they acquiring all their wealth from? Of course, from the government funds that was meant to develop our communities.

We need to come to our turning point, to our senses, and change our thinking pattern if we are to get it right in our beloved country. I therefore urge all citizens to put our individual, instant gratification gained with a token of change aside for the betterment of our dear country.

In Nigeria, we see some in our own country living as second-class citizens. Some are enslaved by obnoxious policies. This is because they want to have their cake, and at the same time, eat it too.

Some Nigerians are moving public funds into their own personal accounts, which were meant for various projects for the development of the country. Yet, they still want to have good roads, good schools, good hospitals, good transportation systems, constant electricity and water, etc. How can you "have your cake and eat it too"? How can you have "the best of both worlds"?

So where is the money going to come from when the nation's funds have been diverted for personal use? Of course, it will no longer be available for the development of the nation.

The only way to have the cake you have already eaten is to vomit the cake, and/or stop eating the cake.

Similarly, the only way to have the money to provide for all these amenities is to surrender it back, or totally stop diverting the money for your own personal use.

When we voted in our dear Mr. President Mohammadu Buhari, we all knew that he was a man of integrity and was willing to work hard to make people-oriented changes for our nation. The president took power without correctly gauging the mood of the nation. However, the president is not a magician, and neither would he be everywhere. Hence, the pillaging goes on unabated. Let us be realistic.

Please empathize and put yourself in our president's shoes!

If I may ask this question: "Where the hell do you want our president to get the money that no longer exists with crumbling economic situations to provide all the above things that every Nigerian wishes to have in the country?" Oil? Trade? Global pandemic barriers?

Now, can we all understand why our president is frustrated and unable to act in line with expectations due to our collective embezzlement?

Our president, I empathize with you. I would not want to be in your shoes. It is similar to having my children stealing all my money. If my children take my money, how am I supposed to pay my bills, feed them, pay their school fees, or clothe and shelter them?

I hope you understand my illustrations, how our luxurious lifestyles, greed, and embezzlement of public monies have made it impossible for our president to perform fully to his sworn role despite the desires of his heart to do so.

To my knowledge, our government seized approximately $153 million from our former Nigeria Petroleum Minister. This is just one person; imagine the combined amounts from all the people that stole our country's money.

Successive governments have squandered the nation's resources until this present administration.

The solemn truth is that corruption among our people has eaten so deeply into the social fabric that it is blamed at all levels of authority.

Some wise words for all of us would be to stop our corruptible attitudes and stop diverting public funds for your own personal use. The attitude is hindering our progress and badly damaging our economy such that we are now at the bottom of most nations.

Nigeria, "a giant of Africa," is now ranked 157th out of 189 countries. This is what our corruptible acidity has landed us.

One of our Nigerian slangs, "Sho, I think dem say warri pikin no dey carry last, how e com be for Naija where una dey come carry last."

Warri pikin you be Nigeria too ooo—if Nigeria is at the bottom, you are at the bottom too ooo. It is the people who make up the nation, including Warri pikin too ooo.

I vividly remember in my form 4 Secondary School, which is equivalent to 10th grade, I ranked in the third position in my class report card, I was so excited to have come third, dancing in the street on my way home. But because in one of my subjects I scored a real low grade, I was scolded and humiliated by my parents.

I've never forgotten this. The first thing I was asked was, "Did the person that came first in your class have more than one head?"

My key point here is that Nigerians strive hard, we are thought to fight for the best, achieve the best. So, how come we are not fighting for our nation? How come we are not the best among other nations in comparison? Similarly, how come we have not channelled this same energy and striving spirit to be the best in our nation too?

Nigerian kids cannot take last positions. We are taught to strive hard and come out on top. Parents get disappointed and surprised when a child comes home as the second best in the class.

Why are Nigerians not channelling this same energy into our beloved country? We are at the bottom of the list among other countries, which is worse than second best. Our disciplined values have become very slack, lacking awareness to the damages our corruptibility has caused us all.

My people, our tongues have been tied for too long about this growing trend of corruption in our society. At the expense of everything in Nigeria, and perhaps not directing the blame to the appropriate quarters, "Let us call a spade a spade." We have some rot amongst us in Nigeria that is not allowing our system to function properly. Corruption has defaced the image of our country and deprived the country of foreign investors who could be willing to do business and develop our tourist potential. These are opportunities that would have created employment in our country and boost our economic growth.

Corruption is similar to pollution in description. Both are harmful to the environment. When released into the atmosphere, these harmful materials are called pollutants. Pollutants can be human activity and damage the quality of air, water, land, etc. Similarly, corruption has damaged our air, water, electricity, land, and roads. I see corruptions as a runoff produced by our selfish people to damage the good and the glory of our economy and land.

Please call a spade a spade.

The annoying part of it all is the blame and finger pointing at everyone. Have you all checked yourselves? Check the extent of your corruptive behaviour on your own little jurisdiction and how these characteristics have impacted us all at large. The remaining nine fingers are surely pointing at us all.

It is fair to demand the basics of what life can offer. But the president cannot do it alone. It has always been a collective effort. When we set an unrealistic goal, the means to achieving the goal may also be unrealistic. No one in this world can achieve national growth alone.

Similarly, a mother of seven may have five of the children stealing from the house—stole almost her entire salary, sold the television, plates, pots, fridge, and stove, and demanded their mother to still take good care of them. Where the hell would she find money to provide for them? The children are complaining of hunger, discomfort, boredom, etc. But they already stole the food money, there is no stove on which to cook meals, and no leisure equipment in the house to entertain them. The mother represents the nation, and we collectively represent the children.

Do you want the president to dip his hands into his pockets to bring out money to feed more than 200 million people? Please, can someone educate me on this, because I do not get it. It is so unreasonable and unjustifiable to put the entire blame on the president for lack of development and security in the nation. Is it not the citizens who collectively mismanaged our common wealth?

As Martin Luther King Jr. rightly intoned, "Law and order exists for the purpose of establishing justice, and when they fail in this purpose, they become the dangerously structured dams that block the flow of social progress" (KeepInspiring.me n.d.).

CHAPTER 6

THE CONCEPT OF POLITICAL STRUCTURE AND ORGANIZATION IN NIGERIA

In our consideration of the collective decadence of the moral and ethical values in Nigeria, we painstakingly reflect on how the conceptualization of the political and structural organization of Nigeria (Federal, State, and local government) patterns have advanced or impeded the development of our great nation or hindered our advancement as a society. These conceptualizations have also contributed to the disintegration of our laws and social order.

Post-independence, Nigeria was organized and administered in confederal and fiscal federalism. It was a regional arrangement where its elected representatives were more accountable to their constituencies. The centre was not made to dictate to the regions. Each region fended for itself, while the centre catered to defence and external relations. 50% of the region's resources or produce were allocated to the centre for that purpose.

But how did we get to where we are today and allow corruption to be seen as a given and acceptable? What laws or legislation or policies were put in place to enslave the national growth? Who was accountable for what, and to which level of authority? Why was the malaise not detected at once or known that it would ruin us as a nation? Whose interest was this arrangement serving, and what prospects exist for change?

Each state of Nigeria is enriched with abundant natural resources, so how did we find ourselves in the predicament that we are in today? Why do we have to import almost all the materials from other countries when we are capable of producing these for ourselves?

Below are the listed mineral and agricultural resources in Nigeria:

- Bitumen – Lagos, Edo, Ondo, Ogun
- Coal – Ondo, Enugu
- Oil and Gas – Akwa Ibom, Abia, Bayelsa, Edo, Delta, Rivers, Imo, Ondo
- Gold – Edo, Ebonyi, Kaduna, Ijesha, Oyo
- Iron Ore – Benue, Anambra, Kogi State, Kwara, Delta State
- Lead and Zinc – Ebonyi, Benue, Ogoja (Cross River) Kano
- Salt – Akwa Ibom, Abia, Ebonyi, Cross River
- Tin – Jos, Bauchi
- Cocoa – Edo, Anambra, Imo, Kwara, Ondo, Ogun, Osun, Oyo, Cross River
- Uranium - Cross River, Bauchi
- Coffee – Kwara, Bauchi, Osun
- Cotton – Katsina, Kano, Niger, Kwara, Sokoto
- Groundnut – Ebonyi, Katsina, Sokoto, Kano, Niger
- Kola Nut – Ogun, Oyo, Osun, Kwara
- Oil Palm – Akwa Ibom, Imo, Anambra, Oyo, Abia
- Plantain – Ogun, Oyo, Osun, Bayelsa
- Rubber – Delta, Cross River, Ogun, Edo
- Sugarcane – Sokoto
- Timber – Edo, Ogun, Delta, Cross River. (Cited, legit.ng)

How can we possess all of these minerals and agricultural resources and still be so poor?

Each state in Nigeria is capable of building their own wealth and contributing positively to the growth and development of the nation.

Nigeria's issue is with the federal central government allocating money to the states and not giving them the autonomy to develop their own revenue bases. The income that would have been generated from each state would have enriched our country and solved a lot of our pain and suffering. Handing money to the state government without allowing them any responsibility is an issue because the federal government ends up smothering the states, thereby diminishing the potential and growth of each state. Ultimately, this leads to the massacre of the nation's economy and creates a very poor and underdeveloped country. This "smothering" done by the federal government does not allow our states to be the independent, strategic thinkers that can formulate their own ideas on revenue generation for their states.

We can compare the system of federal governments hovering over the state's governments to the idea of "helicopter parenting."

A helicopter parent (also called a cosseting parent or simply a cosseter) is a parent who pays extremely close attention to a child's or children's experiences and problems, particularly at educational institutions.

1. Helicopter parents are so named because, like helicopters, they "hover overhead," overseeing every aspect of their child's life constantly.

2. A helicopter parent is also known to strictly supervise their children in all aspects of their lives, including in social interactions (Wikipedia).

Another submission by Merriam Webster defines it as, "A parent who is overly involved in the life of his or her child."

Overbearing parenting produces detrimental effects in the growth and development of children. Similarly, an overbearing federal government system affects the growth and development of each state and Nigeria at large.

This overdone bureaucracy where the states are not empowered and are not taught how to independently generate revenue will only continue to get worse. This is not to judge the federal government, just like we do not judge the helicopter parents—they are simply just protecting the states from having to struggle. However, over-parenting is over-killing the states' potential and their ability to perform.

Our system is similar to catching the fish and handing it over to the state, but not teaching the state how to catch the fish themselves. How can the states learn how to catch fish when they have never been taught?

An old Chinese proverb says, "Give a man a fish, and you feed him for a day. Teach a man to fish, and you teach him to feed for a lifetime."

Teaching the states and allowing the states to develop useful skills will be beneficial to the whole nation. In years to come, it will grow the nation. If you give a man a fish and the fish run out, when he is hungry again, he will come back to you to ask for more fish, but very soon, you will be out of fish; this is what we see in Nigeria today, isn't it? But if you teach him to catch his own fish, you've empowered him and prepared him. When the fish runs out and he is hungry, he will use the skills from his training to go catch his own fish. This is what Nigeria should be: the federal government teaching each state how to utilize their own resources and giving support only when needed.

Hand each state the necessary skill set with accountability in place. The states need long-term solutions, not just the temporary ones. This is not helping the nation.

Even though funds are allocated to the states by the federal government, the citizens of the states do not see the impact of the money in their communities. The funds shared to the state governments are diverted mostly by the political bigwigs for their personal use and not used for the common good of the people.

It is almost similar to a child who has everything being handed over to them on a silver platter and do not work hard for it. In such scenarios they squander the money, just like we are seeing in our nation today because they do not recognize the value.

There is reckless, inconsiderate, non-prioritized spending at all levels of our government. Maybe if they had worked hard to make the money, it would have been different; maybe they would have been more responsible and ensured proper accountability at all levels of government.

Nigerians, we can collectively eradicate this senseless, reckless spending with inspiration and determination.

To start with this new orientation, do not let anyone buy your conscience with a token bribe by someone who has been rampaging our society because it worsens the situation.

Think about it: if this is working, why are we still in a mess today? We are going in circles.

It is time we at all levels check our immoral conduct and demand accountability and close the identified gaps, so we do not continue to contribute to the breakdown of moral values in Nigeria. We share this blame, from the federal level to the state and the local Government Councils, the communities and citizenry.

The United States of America, China, UK, etc. will not solve our problems. They have their own challenges that need to be resolved. They are pretty blessed that they have a political structure on the ground that enables the system to work. Why can't Nigeria go for good governance and institutional reform? It is our nation, and we have all the resources necessary to make it work, but the interest of the ruling political and economic cabal in Nigeria is a cog in the wheel of progress. Let us all get up together with one goal in mind to break down this chain of slavery.

Martin Luther King Jr. stated that, "The best solutions for our community are not going to come from politicians, government or (from other countries). They are going to come from the man or woman you see in the mirror (the man is me and you). One person at a time. One home at a time. One neighborhood at a time". King Jr. further emphasized that, "One of the ways we can truly be free is to maintain an expectation of righteousness within our homes and communities" (KeepInspiring.me. n.d.). At the very core of everything he taught was an uncompromising belief in these values. King Jr. challenged us to understand how we often slay one another daily through gossip, slander, envy, and wrath. He said that we needed a real revolution of values in our nation and in our communities as much as we needed public policy changes.

"Whatever affects one directly, affects all indirectly. (we) can never be what (we) ought to be until (we) are what (we) ought to be. This is the interrelated structure of reality" (KeepInspiring.me. n.d.).

STATE ARRANGEMENT

During their campaigns, many of our politicians promise good governance but when voted in, turn over a bad leaf. Instead of the people reaping the dividends of democracy, they end up being frustrated by their actions and policies and become lords over them.

Between 1999 until the date Nigeria returned to democracy after many years of military regimes, we can identify little in terms of development, education, infrastructure, etc. Many government schools were built, and textbooks, notebooks, and all necessary writing materials were supplied to the schools for the students and pupils for free—classrooms were fully furnished. All this was done by the state government at that time. I can authoritatively say that myself and some of the politicians in various current positions enjoyed our school days. The schools then were called Jakande school in Lagos as it was the former late Lagos State Governor Lateef Kayode Jakande that built and commissioned it, and the building was later modernized by a Military Governor Air Commodore Gbolahan Mudashiru.

Let's take a look at our present schools using Lagos State as a case study.

Oshunrinade O. (2020, Nov 7). "Dilapidated infrastructure, inadequate teachers hinder learning in Lagos public schools". New Telegraph.

Most of them are nothing to write home about. Many do not have chairs and desks for students to sit on, roofs are leaking during the rainy season, and teachers are owed salaries for months and sometimes years of work. Did I hear someone ask about textbooks and notebooks? Hmm—let's not go there.

Most schools with a new facelift are done by the school's alumni association who wanted to give back to the school, since government refuses to play their role, by donating desks, chairs, laboratory equipment, and more. The government does not care about the downturn of our education because none of their children are schooling in the country. Some will send their children to those expensive private schools within and abroad. It should not be like that, because all children are created equal and entitled to the same rights. What is good for our political and religious leaders' children is also good for all our citizens across the nation.

We all deserve quality healthcare, quality housing, well-equipped schools, and the like. Just like Martin Luther King Jr. once mentioned, "No, no, we are not satisfied, and we will not be satisfied until justice rolls down like waters and righteousness like a mighty stream" (KeepInspiring.me. n.d.).

The greatest of all legacies a government can give to their people is good education. The present Joint Admission Matriculation Examination results (2021) confirmed to us that all the level of education have gone down the drain and decayed. For the first time in years, we experienced mass failure beyond belief. Even the Registrar was ashamed to announce the result figures. Seeing the conditions of our schools, the question we should asked ourselves is—where are all the funds assigned to education yearly in the budget?

LOCAL GOVERNMENT ADMINISTRATION

The local government is the third tier of government in Nigeria and is the closest to the people. As a result, it is saddled with many responsibilities. The role of any government and its agencies in societies is highly essential and cannot be overemphasized.

A local government chairman heads the affairs of the local government with the assistance of councillors supporting him. They are elected from the wards that are comprised of 6-10 streets in a local government. It is understood that they know or they are closer to the people, and they are supposed to bring in solutions to the problems of the people and bringing rapid development to the community, but most of these council chairpersons and councillors turned their backs on the people after electing them. They use the council funds to organize very elaborate and extremely expensive parties or Thanksgiving for political visitors. Within a year, they purchase properties worth millions of naira and move away from the people who voted them in. If one is not a party member or doesn't belong to the winning group, then you do not benefit from them. At times, they forcefully use their powers and position to buy people's properties. If you interview these local government councillors about of their roles and duties, many will know that their mindset is getting into that position and getting rich; that is why development is not felt or seen at the grassroots.

EFFECTS OF BAD LEADERSHIP ON THE MASSES

As stated earlier, many of our schoolteachers are not paid their salaries when due—some for months, and others for years. How do you expect them to teach the students efficiently and effectively? Some of the parents cannot afford to buy their children all they need as students, including school uniforms and the like. You see them going to school with torn uniforms, no bags to carry their books, etc. due to their parents not getting paid their salaries. As a result of this, many students find schooling boring, non-encouraging, and unattractive. Some of them start engaging in criminal acts at very tender ages like yahoo yahoo & co. At this early stage in life, they do not believe in studying nor the hard work that leads to success anymore. To them, any means of making money is acceptable, not minding even killing others to get rich. What a bad example the system is teaching the youths.

Due to the lack of checks and balances in the local government's financial dealings, funds meant for the councillor's constituency development are used as personal funds to buy choice properties in their constituencies and communities. Personal revenue tickets are printed by officials of the local government to collect levies from traders in the market and locked-in shops attached to buildings. These duplicated levies are channelled into their personal accounts, not the local government's account.

Funds meant for development, infrastructure, environmental maintenance, and provisioning of clean water is not available. These shameless practices led to the hijacking of the local government council allocations by the state governors, themselves private potentates. This kind of political structure is what is slowing down accountability, and in effect, leading to the moral and ethical decadence in our nation. Physical investigations shows that most people in the local government area who cannot dig borehole in their houses buy water from truck pushers every day because the council has failed in its primary responsibility.

CITIZENS AND CITIZENSHIP

Nigeria is just a mere name. What makes up a nation is its people. Nigeria is not the one that can cause problems—it is the people residing in this country that can. Nigeria cannot fix itself, either. It is up to the people to achieve that.

The questions on my mind is this—what is the salary of the Nigerian local government chairpersons and councillors that they were able to buy properties worth millions within a short period? Why has the Economic and Financial Crimes Commission not investigated these so-called chairpersons and councillors since the formation of the agency?

As a leader, you must be accountable to the people you lead. You have to exhibit the character of a true leader that can be trusted by your followers. We have so much made available to us by God that we can harness and transform our states and local government areas into a modern-day world. We believe strategic planning, hard work, honesty, selfless service, and putting humanity first can make us lead and create a better life for our people and for posterity.

You have to teach people how to treat you—this is what we collectively need now in our nation. Vocalize and show the leaders how you want to be treated.

We are saying that you have power over your actions or reactions. Therefore, if there is a person in your life who is not treating you with the respect and consideration you deserve, you have a decision to make. Are you willing to accept accountability, and do you really want to make a change? If the answer is yes, then you should ask yourself: "What am I doing to elicit this person's behaviour or to allow it to continue?" Even if you think you are not doing anything, your inaction is speaking for you. "Believe in yourself, and believe that you are somebody. Nobody else can do this for us. No document can do this for us. No Proclamation can do this for us. No Civil Rights Bill can do this for us" (KeepInspiring.me. n.d.). That is how Martin Luther King Jr. saw it.

"Courage is an inner resolution to go forward despite obstacles; cowardice is a submissive surrender to circumstances. Courage breeds creativity; cowardice represses fear and is mastered by it. Cowardice asks the question, 'Is it safe?' Expediency asks the question, 'Is it politic?' Vanity asks the question, 'Is it popular? But conscience asks the question, 'Is it right?' There comes a time when we must take a position that is neither safe, nor politic, nor popular, but one must take it because it is right" (KeepInspiring.me. n.d.).

We should not focus or dwell on the immorality and social decay in Nigeria—the deed has been done. We should stop pointing fingers on who did what or not. This is surely not the time, and that is not going to change anything in our land. We cannot go back to the past to change what has happened; there is no point being upset over something that had already happened, but l tell you—it can be changed. However, in hope of redemption, we must collectively push the power buttons to change things for the sake of the future. That is, if we can start focusing on ourselves, our family, our community, our states, and our federal arrangements, starting to do that will change things and restore Nigeria.

It's not right to say Nigeria is a ruined country. Citizenship demands a sense of patriotism from all Nigerians. Please do not join to say that— do not use that bad word on our beautiful country. Nigeria is not ruined. Nigeria is a beautiful country enriched with abundant agricultural and mineral resources. Nigerians, it's time we proudly proclaim positive words on the land; the words that come from our mouths are powerful, and they can damage our image, but the powers of our words can change things too.

If our words contain beauty, people treasure them, and vice versa.

CHAPTER 7

LACK OF ENABLING ENVIRONMENT FOR GROWTH OF INDUSTRY AND DEVELOPMENT

The central theme of this work is about the collective contributions of the Nigerian populace—every citizen at strategic and non-strategic levels, and by citizenship and patriotic requirements or expected behaviour or otherwise in the observed moral and ethical decadence in Nigeria. These value-laden roles are long lost, are seen to have highly complex phenomena and must be investigated to create a relationship for proper understanding of our subject matter in this chapter.

What are the factors inhibiting the growth of industry and development in Nigeria? What is driving or impeding the Nigerian business environment? How does Nigeria as a nation see development in comparable terms with the international or global view? What are the industrial growth trends in Nigeria from independence until now? What is responsible for the capital flight from Nigeria from the 1980s until now? Could we draw inferences from our collective experience and learn anew the winning ways of the developed world?

As can be gleaned, we cannot proffer sufficient answers in this volume, but many more interrelated questions would surely be raised by reasons of our collective responsibilities or failures in arresting this malaise for so long. Naturally, the place of government and its policies as the watchdog of the business environment would not escape the beaming light of investigation.

Because this book is not a critique of the present government in power or indeed the preceding regimes, we are only interested in the roles and collective behaviours inherent in all of us toward the disintegration of the moral and ethical conducts as we input the same in our daily grind in whatever capacities we find ourselves. It is an indictment of the "we."

To start with, let us consider how these factors comes into play and determine the state of disjointed growth we have today. "Throughout history," writes Charles Tilly, "great shifts in the arrangement of power have ordinarily produced and have often depended on exceptional movements of collective violence." Violence, as used here, is a mega concept that encompasses the framing behaviours and conducts of those in authority that determine the structural and physical sufferings as well as the destruction of our crucial life chances. In operation, this is evident in governmental policies and legal frameworks that serve only the interest of a few ruling cabals.

Works on this subject would be justified even if they bring forth one result—to make known the faults and over-simplifications evident in official activity, in public and private declaration, and in the general attitude of those we call honest men. So long as judges set themselves up as dispensers of retribution, so long as judges believe along with the vast majority of public opinion in the deterrent value of punishment, so long as corruption is no longer committed by the police, the industry operators, the military, the prison guards, and in a very special way by the legislators and government, things will get better, but we will still have a lot of work to do.

The environment of going concerns, like the habitat of animals, contributes to their development. Like the natural environment of living things, the environment of a business can either enhance or stifle its growth and development. The nature and extent of the impact of the development on any one company or industry depends on the internal configuration of such a company. Researchers have categorized the environment into three components: macro, industry, and the internal environment, which is the preparedness of any one company. It has also been shown that the internal environment affects performance most, followed by the industry environment, and lastly the macro environment. We shall say more on this in further emphasis.

Nigeria started as a company, the Royal Niger Company, and became a protectorate and finally a republic. As a republic, there were businesses that were run by the government. The government was doing business and also providing the enabling environment for businesses. With this, it became obvious that the government was not a good entrepreneur and that it was better to concentrate on providing an enabling environment while private organizations are allowed to run the business.

This led to the wave of privatizations that is still ongoing. The interplay of government and business, first as a direct participant and later as a provider of an enabling environment, suggests the importance of the environment in the prospects of businesses. It would appear that due to the developing nature of the Nigerian business environment, it is likely to occupy a critical position in the performance of businesses. Using simple Ordinary Lease Square (OLS), the Nigerian business environment and the performance of companies in it was explored (Dogara 2015).

The environment is classified as follows:

- Economic
- Technological
- Socio-cultural
- Political/Legal

Researchers (such as Stoke 2010) are of the opinion that the combination of less controlled external factors together with controllable internal factors arising from personal attributes, management competencies, and behaviour of industry operators are some of what influence the start-up or survival of industries.

After independence, Nigeria was blessed with leaders who had an understanding of developed economies. In the first and second ten-year development plan, we could see an aggressive desire to transform the nation. The first-generation universities, the major highway roads and rail lines connecting Nigeria, and agricultural pursuits were given adequate attention. They remain the glory of those visionary leaders.

The cocoa house in Ibadan and the first television company in black Africa are there in history. The groundnut pyramid in the north and the development of the coal city of Enugu are relics of industry that could have grown and developed. But what led to the collapse of these noble visions are contained in our moral and ethical bankruptcy and driven by a corrupt business environment.

The key factors for consideration include:

- Inadequate infrastructural facilities (road, water, electricity, etc.)
- Insecurity of lives and property
- Inconsistent monetary, fiscal, and industrial policies
- Limited access to markets
- Multiple levels of taxation and levies

- Lack of modern technology for processing and preserving products
- Policy reversals
- Capacity limitations
- Data inadequacies
- Hash operating environment
- Fragile ownership base
- Fragile capital base
- Government policies
- Globalization effects
- Financial institutions
- Local government policies
- Attitude to work
- Endemic corruption in private and officialdom

And the list goes on and on....

Let us take the agricultural sector as an industry that used to provide employment to about 70% of the populace. Why did we abandon it such that we have become a nation unable to feed itself? Why did we choose to import virtually everything?

Malaysia came to Nigeria in the early 1970s and took palm oil seedlings, researched them, and improved the species. Today, that nation is a net exporter of palm oil. What about our cocoa and groundnut? Why has our coffee industry been unable to compete favourably? Incorrect priorities and governmental policies and a poor enabling environment led to the stagnation of these industries.

In Akwa Ibom state, for instance, years of military regimes and policy reversals led to the poor performance of the smelter steel industry, whereas billions of dollars have been spent to develop the steel industry in Ikot Abasi. How can Nigeria take off for proper industrialization if its steel industry remains a veritable source of capital flight and incurable corruption? The same story is recorded at the Ajaokuta Steel Company in Kogi state. The situation remains the same at the Alaja Steel Company in Delta state. When these companies were slated for privatization, what were the modalities for privatization and who were the invisible faces of the investors who bought them? Was due process followed? It is a travesty but also a truism that the wealthy cabals in Nigeria used their powers in government and corruptively fronted syndicates to buy these national assets for their selfish purposes. How did the Nigerian populace rise up to that moral bankruptcy? We became complacent, and the rot goes on.

The National Electric Power Authority (NEPA) and National Telecommunications (NITEL) were both privatized. The national air carrier, Nigerian Airways, also disappeared.

In Akwa Ibom state, Quality Ceramics Limited at Itam, Itu, with plenty of raw materials, also collapsed. Its counterpart, Paper Mill Limited at Oku Iboku, Itu, notable for book production, also failed to prosper. The dry-cell battery industry built by German experts, as well as the biscuit industry in Ikot Ekpene, can only be remembered as industry that could have added to our employment and export capacities. Those factors enumerated above contributed significantly to their non-performance.

In Kano state, the Raleigh company, famous for bicycle assembly, can no longer be seen. The cotton manufacturing industries in the north simply lost their pride and focus because the powers that be turned their attention to the oil industry, and through corrupt military regimes, allocated all known Oil Mineral Lease (OML) licences and marginal fields in the south to themselves. These, of course, breed social, economic, and political upheavals in the region who felt they have been techni-cally removed from what society provides. Today, that region remains a volatile zone waiting to explode.

In Ondo state, the Oluwa glass industry at Igbokoda that was meant to produce windshields for cars and windowpanes for homes has long gone into oblivion. All the factors above contributed.

When we talk about power generation, transmission, and distribution in Nigeria as a critical ingredient for industrialization and growth, we often ask why it is so difficult to generate a paltry 12,000 megawatts when we have huge gas deposits, coal, and hydropower sources? Because of our moral and ethical decadence, this situation of national calamity has been milked by the evil cabals who sees importation of generators from Asia and other countries as a source and opportunity for their wealth, and therefore would frustrate any attempt at freeing the nation from the stranglehold of such dubious business cabals. And these powerful cabals are everywhere in government and in public spheres.

Why are road networks so poor and in many states completely dilapidated? What contractors were used and what quality control or quality assurance and monitoring for efficiencies were put in place? Why are such projects often abandoned with recklessness and without prosecution? In any event, what maintenance policies are put in place to cater to sustainability?

Why have we not thought of a national alternative to each of the transport systems in Nigeria? The air and waterways as well as the railway systems should be maximized in order to take away the burden from our roads and gradually reduce traffic on our major highways.

Let's look at the present realities and insecurities in Nigeria. How did insecurity take centre stage in Nigeria? Who and what fuelled it? Who are these rebels? If they are not Nigerians, who allowed them into the nation with dangerous weapons, and how did they get in? Whose duty was it to man the borders for home security? And, if they are Nigerians, what is the place or contribution of poverty, radicalization, and ideological leanings? Who taught them these ideologies, and why are they offended by the belief systems and practices of others? What is the place of national orientation and education and other intervention platforms in Nigeria? What legal framework was brought to bear with them based on the rule of law?

Today, insecurity thrives. It is a way of making money with powerful sponsors in high places. How can such an environment attract investors and foreign direct investments? Without such an enabling environment, no industry can operate and survive in Nigeria.

Research on the ease of doing business in Nigeria uncovered poor database and internet reliability as well as communications in Nigeria. What level of technology is available to our scientists, and how is research and development treated in Nigeria as a key factor of growth? What is the budgetary allocation for such purposes?

The cost of the federal and state legislature appears too high in Nigeria. Maintaining the status quo essentially and factually depletes the national coffers whereby more people-oriented projects are not executed or even considered.

Each time l visit the famous textile factories around Aswani axis in Lagos, l often wonder why the fabric industry collapsed. We had the raw materials, and we had the manpower. Was it management incompetence, the inability to match modern technology in the industry, or simply the access to funds or a government ban on importation of spare parts for the machineries? Whatever factors that played a part in the folding up of these companies, we are convinced that beyond training and technology, there seems to have been a very poor enabling environment, especially during the long years of military interregnum in Nigeria. And this was an era when corruption was accentuated to the power of ten in Nigeria. The same people kept recycling themselves and their cronies in public offices until today.

Inconsistent fiscal policies continue to contribute to the poor growth of industry in Nigeria. The financial institutions and the Central Bank's inability to stabilize the exchange rate is inhibiting businesses in Nigeria. Yes, Nigeria is a large market, but the limitation of this market has various barriers that only an efficient, enabling environment can remove. How are rural, uneducated women, men, the aged, the poor and invalids targeted? What data and information are presented about this class? What represents their needs, and whose responsibility it is to budget for them and develop an institution or industry to produce their needs? If there are no welfare programs for such, then it is doubtful to believe there exists a future for this unfortunate group in Nigeria.

We need to strengthen the legal and institutional framework for the operation of micro-finance institutions, including tax incentives for micro companies and special incentives targeted at investors who would specialize in exporting to foreign markets and review and implement a codified tax and incentives structure reform that supports large industries to foster growth of micro enterprises in their value and supply chain.

As part of an enabling environment, we may need to provide a targeted tax deductibility incentive for science, technology, and research and development spending. There is a need to design, develop, and implement a fast-track export orientation by harnessing our resources for productive capacities. We can also encourage the creation of industrial estates and clusters of businesses so that allied fields could foster mutual relationships in the growth chain.

Studies aimed at attracting foreign investors, scanning, and overseas markets could be undertaken for special products.

The Bank of Industry and other financial institutions such as Nigerian Exports and Imports Bank (NEXIM), etc. could be strengthened to effectively provide a window of special funding/concessional loan and credit guarantee schemes.

EFFECTS OF GLOBALIZATION

As a member of the international community, Nigeria is not shielded from globalization. However, the country is exposed to both the positive and negative effects of globalization. This chapter, in its analysis of the means for enabling the environment for growth of industry, looks at how this can be harnessed in Nigeria with a balancing effect. It focuses on its impact on science and technology and the environment. It argues that although globalization presents many opportunities, it also exposes developing countries like Nigeria to many new challenges.

The internet is a very powerful tool with two basic, distinct characteristics. The first is that it contains the biggest, richest, and wide-ranging resource of information in the entire world; secondly, it enables people to obtain an interactive mechanism to instantly communicate with each other. It provides a transparent window through which global experiences and best practices are shared. It enables networking, learning, cost savings from trial and error, and avoidance of uncertainties. Knowledge is power, and information is the key to knowledge. Information and Communication Technology (ICT) facilitates data information, transmission, knowledge acquisition, dissemination, and the creation of a value chain. International exchanges act as conduits for knowledge transfer. Knowledge-intensive sectors like education, health, and biotechnology hold promises of phenomenal growth due to the advances in ICT. Developing countries need not recreate costly knowledge—they have the advantage of acquiring and adapting knowledge already available in the richer countries (Jaja 2010).

The world is shifting from a manufacturing-based industrial economy to a service-dominated and network-based knowledge economy (Mohanty 2005:2). ICT is enough of an important catalyst for the transformation of business, society, and government in the globalizing world. Today, ICT forms the "backbone" of several industries, such as banking, airlines, and publishing. It is also an important value-added component of consumer products, such as television, cameras, cars, and mobile telephones. It has facilitated the packaging of information and sending the same across the world at negligible cost.

With the loss of moral and ethical decadence and in a complacent world, human trafficking for commercial sex purposes increased the spread of HIV in Nigeria. Trafficking in persons, which the International Labour Organization (ILO 2001:47) describes as "the underside of globalization," is one of the greatest human rights challenges of our time. A large number of trafficked victims are either kidnapped or lured into following the perpetrators, usually to countries abroad: Italy, Germany, Holland, Belgium, France, and Spain to name a few. The trafficked persons are mainly women and girls and are placed in brothels, private homes, tourist establishments, and street corners where they are forced to offer sexual activities for money. Many of these women often engage in their trade without condoms, and some suffer from HIV and finally die.

Globalization has had a negative impact on the environment through deforestation. According to Wikipedia, globalization is often viewed as a root cause of deforestation. The overuse of natural resources due to increased demand and also the removal of ecosystems due to population growth have had a large negative impact on the environment. Extensive deforestation in the logging industry has occurred worldwide and is being fuelled by the need for disposable products.

There is a need to urgently and effectively address these challenges arising from globalization. Without doubt, globalization is an irreversible process in accordance with natural laws. In as much as the pain caused by some aspects of globalization is undeniable, the real issue is

whether the negative effects of its sweeping processes can be amelio-
rated, and the positive effects enhanced. This is because it is apparent
that globalization has come to stay.

There is a need for Nigerians to preserve their culture in any way
possible. It is a shame that many Nigerian children of this generation
cannot speak their mother tongue or understand their culture. Nigerians
need to exploit the process of globalization to promote their cultures.
For instance, the internet can be employed to propagate the country's
culture. There could be an updated website where the youths could
browse to learn proverbs and the rudiments of their cultures.

Therefore, there is need for a reassessment of how Nigeria has fared
in the era of globalization. Science in a globalizing world has benefits
that Nigeria can and should take advantage of. The era of computers
revolutionized telecommunications, and the internet is what the country
cannot shy away from, but the positives of the times should be properly
harnessed for the country to appropriately benefit from globalization.

Instead of a consolidation of the cultures and values of the country,
various dimensions of globalization continue to erode what makes this
part of the world unique. Imitation and adoption of western values is
happening to the detriment of the nation's essence of existence.

Nigeria needs to figure out how it will not be swallowed by globalization. Instead of total reliance of what the west is handing down,
the country needs to encourage local production and industry. Nigeria
needs to demonstrate her beliefs in indigenous technical knowledge and
skills, instead of being subjected to the mercy of globalization without
being globalized in the real sense of it. The country must be proud of
her heritage and way of life instead of being submerged in the western
way of life. Also, over-dependence on oil, which is also a vehicle driving
globalization, may spell doom for the nation. There is a need for the
return to agriculture as the mainstay of the country's economy. By doing

so, it will reduce the dependence of the country on the western world. The existing government policy and regulation in the management and control of e-waste in Nigeria is inadequate and insufficient for proper management. There is a need for the government to pass safety laws to restrict and limit the flow of hazardous substances and discarded electronics into Nigeria. More so, only electronics manufactured by companies who comply with the non-toxic components requirement and those with details informing consumers about the chemicals used should be allowed into Nigeria. Lack of data on the volume of e-waste imported into the country or generated domestically constitutes a primary concern for a proper enabling environment for the growth of industry in a globalized world.

CHAPTER 8

SELFISH AMBITIONS

According to Meriam-Webster, selfishness is being concerned excessively or exclusively for oneself or one's own advantage, pleasure, or welfare regardless of others. Or, as Oscar Wilde once said, "Selfishness is not living as one wishes to live; it is asking others to live as one wishes to live."

Nigerians went astray, deviating away from the right path and direction of moral and ethical values in the process of outsmarting, being competitive for the most riches in order not to fail, and disappointing or putting to shame, since our societies classify richness with success.

In the process of striving hard for wealth and pleasing the community that will appraise them, they got lost, forgetting about everything else around them except the focused mindset of luxurious life. They become so fixated on their characters and thought processes that it hindered them to work together to help the nations grow. All they are thinking about is their own growth and monopolizing everything around them.

While some of our Nigerians in the positions of power are ruthlessly striving for richness, other Nigerians are hurt, in pain, and suffering, not recognizing how these self-centred actions have affected all to a higher degree of frustration. As we have seen in Nigeria, self-obsession has robbed us all of happiness, and it has helped to collapse the entire nation.

According to one of the laws of God to mankind is to love our neighbours as ourselves. An average American will be thinking of what they will do for their country; Nigerians are busy thinking of what the country will do for them. Americans call their country a dream, while Nigerians call theirs a piece of cake, meaning when you have the opportunity to gain a post in the government, one goes there to cut his or her part of the cake, thereby milking down the country.

Selfishness among our politicians in positions—either voted in or appointed—destroys many government infrastructures meant to be of great value to the public and development of the nation, money meant to build or develop our hospital to standards are being diverted to private accounts, all because they and their family members can easily travel abroad for medical treatment. Contracts are issued to family members who are not qualified, and politicians do not even care if the contracts are being executed as long as the larger part of the contract funds ends up in their account.

Our educational institution is drowning year in, year out because of selfishness in the minds of the people appointed to develop it. Money meant to pay for teachers' and lecturers' salaries and upgrades to facilities are not available to the right sectors, leading to students not getting the right quality of education needed. They could care less if the students have good and qualified teachers, care less if they have enabled a quality teaching environment; many of the secondary schools have no chairs or desks, no textbooks in the library compared to what we had in the days of our late Lagos State Governor Pa Lateef Kayode Jakande when books and textbooks were available for all students with a good learning environment and teachers were paid salaries at the right time. Many of them benefited from these same government schools while growing up. Now, they could care less because their children are not schooling here; rather, they send their children to a well-furnished and standard school abroad with taxpayers' money kept in their custody. Why would a man with so many properties want to convert another man's property because he's a legislator; this happened in one of the local governments in Lagos State last year. It's nothing but selfishness. This man would not have been a legislator if he had not benefited from the standard of education they enjoyed during the time of the late pa Lateef Jakande, but today they cannot give the same back to the younger generations. I know a prominent Nigerian whose name can never be erased easily in Nigeria, not because of his wealth but because he is a symbol of love to the whole nation. He wasn't self-centred; rather, his wealth touched across the whole part of the country, and that was why he was able to win in all the states including the territory of his opponent in the 1993 presidential election that was cancelled—M.K.O. ABIOLA. Today, every June 12, he is being remembered.

On to our youths, many of our youths now don't believe education is the key to success as we were made to believe many years back. *Ti o ba ka iwe bata re adun kokoka*—meaning, if you read your books, you were assured of a better life, but their selfish ambition of getting rich quick has resulted into many of them doing yahoo yahoo, an escalating money ritual—they can kill their fathers, mothers, sisters, brothers, neighbours, and strangers. Kidnapping and banditry, to them, is the best job.

I remember reading an article that illustrates the rate of selfishness in Nigeria:

> A Nigerian man was given the opportunity to ask for anything he wanted. The condition was that, whatever he got, his brother would receive double. He thought about asking for a house, but he didn't like the thought of his brother having two houses. So, he thought about asking for a million dollars to go to his bank account; but again, he was unhappy with the thought of his brother having two million dollars in his account. The man sat down and thought hard. 'What can I have and still be better than

my brother when he has double?' So, he thought of having one of his eyes removed so that his brother might have his two eyes gouged.

This is the typical mentality that has set Nigerians backward for ages and has caused witchcraft to thrive in Nigeria.

When most Nigerian men succeed, they want to enslave their brothers; they try to make the class gap between them and their brothers widen daily. All this has started from our parenting. Instead of parents teaching their children to study to become better people, they teach them to become better than somebody else's children, thereby creating unnecessary competition when parents buy new clothes for their children and give rags to their maids taking care of the children and the home.

The act of selfishness has made the whole nation unsafe and has destroyed the image of the nation internally and externally.

No doubt, there is no way that Nigeria can be restored without removing the total selfishness and self-centred ambitions and putting a stop to all the bad stuff we are doing.

Let us all understand that SELFISH AMBITIONS lead to teaching fables instead of truth, dishonest gains, and exploitation.

Do not let SELFISH men or greedy interests strip our country of its beauty, its riches, or its romance –Theodore Roosevelt

CHAPTER 9

POLITICAL VIOLENCE

Violence is recognized as a form of aggression. The reaction of every individual to the same situation can be different, though. Thus, short-tempered persons and those who are not able to put a halt on their emotions because of the environment that constantly changes usually behave irrationally. They feel frustrated, which becomes a reason for anger and causes violent behaviour.

Let us look at the meaning of "violence" according to the World Health Organization (WHO):

> "The intentional use of power or physical force threatened or actual, against oneself, another person or against a group or community that either results in or has a high likelihood of resulting in injury, death, psychological harm, mal-development or deprivation."

Since the beginning of democracy in Nigeria in 1999, our politicians have engaged thugs mainly to cause violence among their party members and opponents.

In Nigeria, people boast about violence, power, and money. As a result, people use violence to obtain public funds from time to time. This works for some people, hence other people in the community want to use the same violence to acquire public funds too. The effects of violence on our youths constitute idle minds and boredom due to lack of jobs, and many turn to violence to make money due to poverty in the nation, etc.

The aspirations to acquire power and be wealthy in politics has given birth and contributed to political violence in Nigeria. Political violence has destabilized our democracy. Nigeria is a democratic country, but a lot of politicians are turning it into an authoritarian nation through political thuggery. They want power by any means because power will generate funds and provide luxurious lifestyles, not minding who is affected, injured, and displaced due to their longing for money—violence to acquire money by any means. As a result, they took advantage of vulnerable Nigerian people who have no job or source of livelihood, buying firearms, explosives, and all manners of weapons for them to destroy the peace and co-existence of Nigerians. Initially, politicians used these thugs to intimidate their political opponents, promising these people job positions, luxurious lifestyles, and government contracts as rewards. That is the reason that many political assassinations occur during a year of elections—engaging thugs to threaten opponents and even voters who they felt are not willing to vote for them.

As a result of the violence our politicians have engaged in, much has been destroyed; the weapons they bought for those thugs during their political campaigns to threaten opponents have not been returned, and in turn these thugs now use those weapons after elections have been won and lost to commit crimes. Presently, Nigeria is tagged as the most unsecured nation in the world due to kidnapping, banditry, armed robbery, and so on. Some kidnappers confessed after being arrested that the AK-47 guns they possessed were given to them by the politicians during elections, and when money wasn't forthcoming after the elections, they had to make use of the guns to make money. While using other people's children for violent behaviours or other families for the destruction of the nation, their children are safe, with some abroad attending school in a non-violent nation.

Nigerian people must all refuse to be used for violent acts to destroy their own nation. We must all say NO to violence if we are going to have a better society and develop our country.

Many Nigerians have lost interest and confidence in the politics of Nigeria as a result of violent activities that occur to secure power. During an election, many are afraid to come out to exercise their rights. Our elections, that are meant to be peaceful, have become bloody because of our greediness to acquire money.

It is time to enlighten our politicians; the thugs they engaged and the weapons they bought for them are now creating unrest in the country. There's an old adage that says, "If you live in a glass house, do not throw stones," and also, "If you throw a stone into the market, it might be your family member in the market that the stone will hit." Most of the children or people that these people-turned-kidnappers are kidnapping are the wealthy in the community—the politicians and their families are not left out.

I believe once a problem is identified, a rapid solution can be taken. We all should partake in solving this violence in our communities and nation at large.

CHAPTER 10

INGRATITUDE AND DISCONTENTMENT

How do these two terms add up to define the central theme of this book, namely the ethical and moral decadence prevalent in Nigeria? To come to terms, there must be an understanding of what drives men, institutions, and processes.

Having lived in both ends of the world in developed and under-developed countries, I have seen that some people living in developed countries sometimes do not appreciate what they have. I have seen a lot of ingratitude from citizens' behaviour.

Sometimes I wish this case could be reversed with a trans-residential swap. Only in this way would Nigerians understand how lucky they have been and recognize the daily overflow of human discontentment and ingratitude of our leaders and citizens.

Do our leaders show gratitude to God Almighty for the land and the numerous economic and human resources with which we have been blessed? How are these managed for the common wealth of the nation? In spite of many centuries of colonial exploitation and the rapid desire to build a nation, have the leadership shown a contentment that years of fraud and deprivations ought to give way for the commonality of our people? Why have we not used our diversity for profitable advantage?

Who is benefiting from the sleaze and madness? Discontentment, they say, leads people to the wrong ways. In other countries, these has been harnessed for a positive effect.

For those who have lived in the developed world all of their lives: now imagine a life with no sanitary water to drink, no welfare to support people struggling financially, no way to feed the family, no good roads, and government employees who owe sometimes more than six months. You leave home for work three hours before your shift starts due to heavy traffic that you might encounter on your way, and you get stuck in traffic for about five hours after an eight-hour work day on your way home. You get home, and it is all darkness due to lack of electricity.

Frustration is abundant as there is no functional healthcare system and a poor educational system for your children. Pensions are not paid to our retiree parents who now depend on us to support them, in addition to our siblings, by paying for their upkeep, educational fees, etc. To make matters worse, sometimes you have not even received salary for the preceding six months. Discontent is sure to set in.

If we may ask—how does all this make us feel? What policies and/or laws were put in place? Whose responsibility was it to do what, how, when, and where?

How do they live in such situations? How are they even surviving? Good questions to ponder! This will bring people down psychologically. People will be frustrated, angry, and hopeless, and the cup of human sorrow overflows daily.

In my opinion, I feel that it is crucial to lose something dear to us sometimes so that we might appreciate what we have and be grateful for it.

The problem is that many people do not realize this until it has happened and the added pent-up burden is upon us.

The citizens of the developed world should sometimes appreciate what they have and be grateful to their governments for the provisions put in place for them. One man's meat is another man's poison.

What the developed countries are moaning about and not appreciating is the exact comfort the Nigerians are begging for and will do anything to have. What an irony of life!

My point from the beginning is that, in the developed world, let us be grateful to and support our government in whatever ways we can to make things continue to run smoothly. We should be thankful for the thousands of welfare packages and security and protection the government have provided for its citizens.

On the other hand, in Nigeria, the people you have entrusted to protect your rights and provide for the nation are the same people abusing it. It is sad and deeply hurtful.

When you elect people to a position, you are asking them to advocate and adjudicate in the representative capacity by which they were elected by the people in a political unit, or at the state or federal level.

A considerate representative will be loyal and will advocate and represent their own constituents for that trust bestowed on them. But sadly, due to lack of contentment, they do the opposite for their own interest instead of the interest of the people that voted them in power.

Contentment may be considered to be a satisfaction with what one possesses. A contented person will not go against the law to possess unknown wealth. Although human wants are many and varied, the resources to satisfy them are limited. That means acquiring wealth should be done through proven and honest channels. Contentment is deriving satisfaction in one's situation socially, psychological, and mentally. Contentment means being satisfied with one's possessions, wealth, or situation. Nothing else will be significant or matter to you because you are satisfied with what you have.

A contented person is one who becomes aware that contentment starts with a satisfied mind and a gratuitous heart. A contented person is not looking or longing for more. Lack of contentment among our leaders have led them to the brutal mismanagement of our public funds to dehumanize us, to destroy our children children's future, and to bring our nation to the worst humiliation. You can strive for more success so long as you work hard and earn it properly.

Having success at the expense of others is what has brought the nation to the present decadence. It is not right and is classified as immorality. Kindly put others into those shoes too. Think about if you are on the receiving end. How will you feel? This is why we have to learn to empathize.

A great man named Napoleon Hill once said, "Success is the ability to acquire whatever one wants, without violating the rights of others." In the case of Nigerians, they are acquiring their successes and so-called wealth at the expense of the entire nation and hence violating citizens' rights. Sometimes this can be fatal to the people, and nothing is being done to stem the tide. I shed tears. Anyone who knows what is going on in Nigeria in terms of greediness, lack of contentment, and its effects on the entire nation will no doubt shed tears too.

People strive to survive. Populations are hungry, children are sick, and school dropouts are increasing. Some are being kidnapped and killed. People are dying from preventable childbirth cases. Peoples are dying everyday as result of enormous amounts of embezzlement in the polity. Where is the fear of God in our hearts? Where are our consciences and how do we sleep at night, knowing our actions have caused people structural violence?

How?! Our actions have led so many people to go to bed hungry. Many have died from health challenges, children have dropped out of school, and children have been kidnapped, raped, and traumatized to death.

Close your eyes and take a deep breath. Then, imagine children being kidnapped, the fear on their faces and voices yelling to their parents as they are raped and killed.

Imagine, too, a mother during childbirth, taking her last breath. Imagine a fatal accident on our bad roads, and someone taking a last breath.

This is the consequence of discontentment triggered by greediness, nepotism, and corruption. Discontentment creates an avenue for stealing, corruption, jealousy, greed, unhealthy rivalry, bribery, cheating, and nonchalant attitudes. Lack of contentment and longing for more and more wealth among our elected leaders has caused us to drift from the path of honour and integrity.

Discontentment has radically pushed our moral ethos, norms, and ethical values beyond the precipice.

Contentment is a moral value-add that all citizens of a nation must possess. It is a good characteristic that will help to develop a nation, leaving a legacy for generations yet unborn.

Ingratitude is seen in many climes and in officialdom. Government will delineate a market space and fit in some stores, yet citizens will abandon the markets and prefer to sell on the main roads, causing heavy traffic problems. How do you explain that? Ingratitude.

Flyover bridges are built to aid traffic and saves lives, yet citizens will break the barricades and chose to run across the road filled with fast-moving vehicles. Ingratitude.

Streetlights are meant for safety at night, aesthetics, and illumination. Cables thus laid are mischievously stolen by criminals. What is that? Ingratitude.

Sea port workers are employed by the government and design tasks to add to the ease of doing business, and instead of clearing the goods such as the components of imported cars, appliances, and even quantities of foreign rice, they are surreptitiously removed. How does this add to economic growth for the common wealth? Until such dubious elements are caught and sacked, a sense of gratitude would not lighten up their ways. And the various ways go on. Who will save us from this level of nothingness?

How many citizens pay tax correctly these days? How much of these taxes are truthfully channelled for national development? Have we ever thought of the ingratitude to God for giving us such a huge population and market that could be harnessed for our advantage?

Why are we ungrateful as a nation and as a people? Why do we exploit one region and use the proceeds to build and develop others? Why do we make laws and sponsor bills that profit a few against the ratchet of the earth?

It is ingratitude that has denied us the opportunity to see one another in love as God intended. How can we therefore cooperate and create synergies that abide in national growth?

It is our belief that contentment and gratitude toward God, nation, and humanity will create a pathway for our collective consciousness against the prevailing moral and ethical decadence in the nation.

CHAPTER 11

ACCOUNTABILITY

It is true that a country cannot experience real development if government does not create or give support to small enterprise development in the country, and it's more dangerous if government doesn't have the oversight to look deeply into the accounts of these funds put into the sector.

Accountability is a concept that is crucial to the successful implementation of policies and programs of companies and government by its workers and officials. It is seen as a condition in which individuals who exercise government powers are constrained to act in accordance with the rules and regulations (Chardler & Plano 1988). In this country of ours, the Nigerian government establishes and funds agencies and industries, but with no proper checks and balances. Every year budgets are being allocated to ministries to execute projects, but most projects cannot be accounted for at the end of the year; yet more funds will be allocated the following year without proper accountability for the previous one.

Most of the largest budgets since 1999 have gone to Nigerian National Petroleum Corporation (NNPC) through the Minister of Petroleum, yet none of our refineries are working at more than 50% capacity and fuel is being imported from our small neighbouring countries. Recently, $130 million dollars, $14.4 million worth of jewels, and 80 properties were recovered from the former Minister of Petroleum. If all of these monies were utilized on our refineries, imagine what the state of our refineries would be now.

Development of any society is meant to enhance the living standards of the citizens; however, where there are challenges in accountability, development is more likely to be a mirage. Studies in Nigeria on the challenges of leadership and sustainable development identifies corruption and the lack of required skills on the part of public policy formation and implementation.

In a bid to achieve sustainable development in a society, projects are put in place as a strategy to realize the developmental goals of government. Government spends a huge amount of money on transportation, yet our roads are not drivable. In some parts, potholes have turned to deathtraps, and some criminals picks these areas as their point of operations and the ministers are not called for questioning—even when they do, it is always inconclusive, just like what we received in the early months of 2021 when the upper house of the national assembly called on the NDDC to give accounts on their spending. It was discovered that plastic chairs said to be bought for billions of naira are still in the manufacturer's warehouse. Contracts fully paid for are not executed, and we were led to understand by the minister that most of the contracts in question are collected by some of the seated senators, and that was how the probing ends, just like a movie. Nobody is being prosecuted for incorrect accountability, and the movie continues.

Poor leadership in the various levels of government, poor resource management, poor maintenance culture, and unethical behaviour are challenges against accountability.

We all need to realize and accept that accountability in good governance is the acknowledgement and assumption of responsibility for actions, products, decisions, and policies. This includes the administration, governance, and implementation within the scope of the role or employment position, and encompassing the obligation or report and be answerable.

Funds allocated to other levels of government are really not spent on projects meant for development because they are not accountable for it. What will a councillor account for after he has spent most of the money on personal issues rather than projects to develop his constituency, and who is he accountable to? Is it the top officials that are likely to have removed about 20% of the allocated fund before it reached the councillor?

For the record, the present administration has spent a large sum in development of the nation. Below are some of the achievements after six years with better accountability:

FINANCING

- Presidential approval in 2020 for the establishment of InfraCo Plc, a world-class infrastructure development vehicle, wholly focused on Nigeria, with combined debt and equity take-off capital of $15 trillion and managed by an independent infrastructure fund manager.
- Establishment in 2020 of the Presidential Infrastructure Development Fund (PIDF), with more than $1 billion in funding so far.
- The Nigerian Sovereign Investment Authority (NSIA) has seen a total additional influx from the government of approximately US $2 billion under the Buhari Administration—since the original US $1 billion that the fund kicked off with in 2012.
- Launch of the Nigeria Innovation Fund by the NSIA to address investment opportunities in the domestic technology sector: data networking, datacenters, software, Agri-tech, Biotech, etc.

RAIL

- 156-km Lagos-Ibadan Standard Gauge Rail nearing completion.
- 327-km Itakpe-Warri Standard Gauge Rail completed and commissioned 33 years after construction began.
- Abuja Light Rail completed in 2018.
- Ground-breaking completed for the construction of Kano-Maradi Standard Gauge Rail, and revamp of Port-Harcourt-Maiduguri Narrow Gauge Rail.
- Financing negotiations ongoing for the Ibadan-Kano Standard Gauge Rail project.

ROADS

- Presidential Infrastructure Development Fund (PIDF), investing over a billion dollars in three flagship projects: Lagos-Ibadan Expressway, Second Niger Bridge, and Abuja-Kaduna-Zaria-Kano Expressway.
- Executive Order 7 mobilizing private investment into the development of key roads and bridges like Bodo-Bonny in Rivers and Apapa-Oshodi-Oworonshoki-Ojota in Lagos.
- Highway Development and Management Initiative (HDMI), a public-private partnership program to mobilize, in its first phase, over a trillion naira in private investment into the development and maintenance of twelve Roads, amounting to 1,963 km in length.
- More than 360 billion naira worth of Sukuk Bonds raised since 2017 for dozens of critical road projects across all six geopolitical zones.

PORTS

- Completion of New Terminals for International Airports in Lagos, Abuja, Kano, and Port Harcourt.
- Construction of a new runway for Abuja and Enugu International Airports.
- Presidential approval for four International Airports as Special Economic Zones: Lagos, Kano, Abuja and Port Harcourt.
- Approval for new private-sector-funded deep-sea ports: Lekki Deep-Sea Port (construction already well underway, expected completion in 2022); Bonny Deep-Sea Port (ground-breaking completed in March 2021); Ibom Deep-Sea Port; and Warri Deep-Sea Port.

DEVELOPMENT OF CAPACITY AT THE EASTERN PORTS:

- In December 2017, Calabar Port commenced export of bulk cement to Tema Port in Ghana.
- In 2019, three container ships berthed at Calabar Port for the first time in eleven years.
- Dredging of Warri Port (Escravos Bar—Warri Port channel) completed in 2018.
- On October 30, 2019, an LPG Tanker operated by NLNG, berthed in Port Harcourt—the first time ever an LPG ship berthed in any of the Eastern Ports.
- On December 8, 2019, Onne Port received JPO VOLANS (owned by Maersk), the FIRST gearless and largest container vessel (265.07 metres) to call at any Eastern Port in Nigeria.
- On August 1, 2019, Onne Port's Brawal Terminal received MSC GRACE, its first container vessel since 2012.

POWER

- Energizing Education Programme: Taking clean and reliable energy (solar and gas) to Federal Universities and Teaching Hospitals across the country.
- Four Universities completed and commissioned already: BUK (Kano), FUNAI (Ebonyi), ATBU (Bauchi) and FUPRE (Delta); others ongoing.
- Energizing Economies Programme: Taking clean and reliable energy (solar and gas) to markets across the country. Completed projects include Sabon-Gari Market in Kano, Ariaria Market in Aba, and Sura Shopping Complex in Lagos.
- National Mass Metering Programme: Nationwide rollout of electricity meters to all on-grid consumers, launched in August 2020. The Central Bank of Nigeria is providing 60 billion naira for the first phase, with a target of 1 million metre installations. So far, more than 500,000 metres have been delivered to the Discos, and more than 280,000 installed.
- Solar Power Naija: Launched in April 2021 to deliver 5 million off-grid solar connections to Nigerian households. The program is expected to generate an additional $7 billion increase in tax revenues per annum and $10 million in annual import substitution. In May 2021, the Rural Electrification Agency announced the planned deployment of solar-powered grids to 200 Primary Health Centres (PHC) and 104 Unity Schools nationwide.
- Presidential Power Initiative (PPI), aka Siemens Power Program: A Government-to-Government initiative involving the Governments of Nigeria and Germany, and Siemens AG of Germany to upgrade and modernize Nigeria's electricity grid. Contract for the pre-engineering phase of the Presidential Power Initiative (PPI) was signed in February 2021, following

the 2020 approval for the payment of FGN's counterpart funding for that phase.

- Nigeria Electrification Project (NEP) has provided grants for the deployment of 200,000 Solar Home Systems, impacting one million Nigerians. The NEP is also delivering mini-grids across the country.

HOUSING

- The Family Homes Fund Limited (FHFL), incorporated by the federal government of Nigeria in September 2016, is the implementing agency for the Buhari Administration's National Social Housing scheme.

- More than two thousand (2,000) hectares of land with titled documents have been given by twenty-four States for the Buhari administration's Social Housing programme, with the capacity to accommodate about 65,000 new homes.

- Under the National Social Housing programme, Nigerians will be given at least a 15-year period with a monthly payment at 6 percent interest rate, to pay for each housing unit. The Central Bank of Nigeria is providing a N200 Billion financing facility, with a guarantee by the FGN.

OIL AND GAS

The Buhari Administration has declared this decade the "Decade of Gas."

- Ground-breaking on 614-km Ajaokuta-Kaduna-Kano Gas Project.

- Successful completion of Nigeria's first Marginal Field Bid Round in almost 20 years, expected to raise in excess of half a billion dollars and open up a new vista of investment in oil and gas.

- Launch of National LPG Expansion Programme (including Removal of VAT from the domestic pricing of LPG).
- Financial close and signing of contract for NLNG Train 7, which will grow Nigeria's production capacity by about 35%.
- Nigeria and Morocco have in 2021 signed an agreement to develop a US$1.4 billion multipurpose industrial platform (Ammonia and Di-Ammonium Phosphate production plants) that will utilize Nigerian gas and Moroccan phosphate to produce 750,000 tons of ammonia and 1 million tons of phosphate fertilizers annually by 2025. It will be located in Ikot-Abasi, Akwa Ibom State.
- Commissioning in December 2020 of the new NPDC Integrated Gas Handling Facility in Edo State, the largest onshore LPG plant in the country, with a processing capacity of 100 million standard cubic feet of gas daily, producing 330 tonnes of LPG, 345 tonnes of propane, and 2,600 barrels of condensate daily.
- Establishment of a $350 million Nigerian Content Intervention Fund to finance manufacturing, contracts, and assets in the oil and gas industry.

FINANCIAL CLOSE ON THE FOLLOWING NNPC-INVOLVED PROJECTS:

- A 10,000 ton per day methanol plant and a 500 million standard cubic feet per day gas processing plant, in Odeama, Brass, Bayelsa State.
- The ANOH gas processing plant, with a processing capacity of 300 million standard cubic feet of gas, in Imo State. It is a Joint Venture between Seplat Petroleum Development Company

and the Nigerian Gas Company, a wholly owned subsidiary of NNPC. It also has the potential to deliver 1,200MW of power when completed.

- Comprehensive rehabilitation of the Port Harcourt Refinery (PHRC). Sign-off ceremony of Engineering, Procurement & Construction (EPC) Contract held in April 2021, marking the commencement of site handover and full mobilization to site.

- Policy, Regulatory, and Funding Support for the establishment of Modular Refineries across the Niger Delta. When the administration took office in 2015, Nigeria had only one functioning Modular Refinery. Today there are at least six ongoing brownfield and greenfield Modular Refinery Projects across the Niger Delta. In 2020, President Buhari commissioned the first phase of the Waltersmith Modular Refinery in Imo State.

- Launch of the Nigerian Upstream Cost Optimization Programme (NUCOP) to reduce operating expenses through process enhancement and industry collaboration.

AGRICULTURE

- Anchor Borrowers Program (ABP): The Anchor Borrowers Programme (ABP) of the Central Bank of Nigeria launched by President Muhammadu Buhari on November 17, 2015, has made more than 300 billion naira to more than 3.1 million smallholder farmers of twenty-one different commodities (including rice, wheat, maize, cotton, cassava, poultry, soy beans, groundnut, fish), cultivating over 3.8 million hectares of farmland.

- Presidential Fertilizer Initiative: Launched as a government-to-government partnership between the Nigerian and Moroccan Governments, in December 2016, the Presidential Fertilizer Initiative (PFI) produced ~12 million 50-kg bags of NPK

20:10:10 equivalent in 2020, bringing the total production since inception to over 30 million 50-kg bags equivalent; and number of participating blending plants increased to forty-four from three at inception.

- Special-Agro Industrial Processing Zones (SAPZ) Programme: A partnership between FGN, AfDB Group, and other stakeholders including IFAD and BOI. Under the SAPZ programme, agro-processing centres will be established across the country. The agro-processing centres will be provided with basic infrastructure such as water, electricity, and roads as well as facilities for skills training. Seven (7) States and the FCT selected for the pilot phase, due to commence 2021: Ogun, Oyo, Imo, Cross River, Kano, Kaduna, Kwara.

- The Green Imperative—a Nigeria-Brazil Agricultural Mechanisation Programme aimed at boosting agricultural production in Nigeria. The National Assembly has approved a loan for the financing of the program, which will involve the development of 632 privately-operated primary production (mechanisation) Service Centers and 142 Agro-processing (value addition) service Centres across the 774 LGAs, and the reactivation of 6 privately owned partially operational or moribund tractor assembly plants nationwide. It will also train 100,000 new extension workers.

SOCIAL INVESTMENT AND POVERTY ALLEVIATION

- In 2016, President Buhari launched the National Social Investment Programme, currently the largest such programme in Africa and one of the largest in the world. Currently, the National Social Register of poor and vulnerable Nigerians

(NSR) has 32.6 million persons from more than 7 million poor and vulnerable households, identified across 708 local government areas, 8,723 wards and 86,610 communities across the 36 states of the country and the FCT.

- From this number, 1.6 million poor and vulnerable households (comprising more than 8 million individuals, in 45,744 communities from 5,483 Wards) of 557 LGAs in 35 states and the FCT are currently benefiting from the Conditional Cash Transfer (CCT) program, which pays a bimonthly stipend of $10,000 naira per household.

- In January 2019, President Buhari launched Nigeria's Micro-Pension Scheme – which allows self-employed persons and persons working in organizations with less than 3 employees to save for the provision of pension at retirement or incapacitation.

- Establishment of Survival Fund, National Youth Investment Fund, and National Special Public Works Program (774,000 beneficiaries across 774 LGAs nationwide), and the Central Bank's Covid-19 300 billion Naira Targeted Credit Facility (TCF)—more than 150 billion Naira disbursed so far—to support millions of small businesses, households, and young people, with federal grants, loans, and stipends.

- The Buhari Administration's Survival Fund has provided its grants (Payroll Support, Artisan and Transport Sector grants, and General MSME grants) to more than 800,000 beneficiaries since the last quarter of 2020. It has also provided free business registration to more than 200,000 MSMEs across the country.

- Presidential approval for the establishment of the Nigeria Investment and Growth Fund (NIG-Fund), in 2021.

- As at the end of 2020, Development Bank of Nigeria (which commenced operations in 2017) had disbursed 324 billion naira in loans to more than 136,000 MSMEs, through 40 Participating Financial Institutions (PFIs). (57% of the beneficiaries are women-owned MSMEs while 27% are youth-owned).
- Bank of Industry has disbursed more than 900 billion Naira in loans to over 3 million large, medium, small, and micro enterprises since 2015.

EDUCATION AND HEALTH

- Since assuming office, the Buhari Administration has committed more than $1.7 trillion of capital intervention to Nigeria's tertiary institutions, through various means, including TETFund – with the universities taking the lion share of the total amount.
- The federal government has disbursed more than 170 billion naira in UBE Matching Grants to States and the FCT since 2015, 8 billion naira in Special Education Grant to States and private providers of Special Education, and 34 billion naira from the Teachers Professional Development Fund to States and the FCT.
- Launch of the Alternate School Programme (ASP), designed to ensure that every out-of-school child in Nigeria gains access to quality basic education, irrespective of social, cultural, or economic circumstance, in line with the aspirations of Sustainable Development Goal 4 (SDG-4).
- Presidential approval for a new (extended) Retirement age of 65 and Length of Service of 40 years for Teachers in Public Basic and Secondary Schools in Nigeria (both effective January 1, 2021), as well as a new Special Teachers Salary Scale (effective

January 1, 2022), and also a new Special Teachers Pension Scheme.

- Reduction in number of out-of-school children, by 3,247,590, as of 31st December 2020, achieved through a World Bank-financed program known as 'Better Education Service Delivery for All' (BESDA). 1,792,833 of that number achieved through formal schools while 1,454,757 are through non-formal interventions such as Almajiri, Girl-Child, Nomadic/Migrant and IDPs Education).

- Under the World Bank-supported Innovation Development & Effectiveness in the Acquisition of Skills (IDEAS) Project, approved in 2020, US $200 million will be invested in six participating States (Abia, Benue, Ekiti, Gombe, Kano, Edo) as well as twenty Federal Science and Technical Colleges nationwide. Implementation will be stepped-up in 2021 to afford millions of Nigerian youths the opportunity to acquire hands-on skills to effectively contribute to national development.

Presidential approval for the establishment of the following:

- Federal Maritime University, in Delta State.
- Nigerian Army University, in Borno State.
- Six new Colleges of Education (one per geopolitical zone: Odugbo, Benue State; Isu, Ebonyi State; Ekiadolor, Edo State; Gidan Madi, Sokoto State; Jama'are, Bauchi State; and Iwo, Osun State).
- Six new Federal Polytechnics in Kaltungo, Gombe State; Ayede, Oyo State; Daura, Katsina State; Shendam, Plateau State, Ohodo, Enugu State; and Ugep, Cross River State.
- Under the phased implementation of the National Youth Policy, 6 Federal Science & Technical Colleges (FSTC) were established

in 2020, as follows: FSTC Ogugu, Kogi State; FSTC Hadeija, Jigawa State; FSTC Umuaka, Imo State; FSTC Igangan, Oyo State; FSTC Ganduje, Kano State; FSTC, Amuzu, Ebonyi State. Five (5) additional FSTC will come on-stream in 2021, and will be located in Bauchi, Plateau, Sokoto, Enugu and Cross River States.

- Grants to State Governments: At least $2.5 million disbursed to each State of the Federation and the FCT, under the Saving One Million Lives (SOML) initiative, to improve health outcomes.

- Basic Health Care Provision Fund (BHCPF): For the first time since the National Health Act was passed in 2014, the Federal Government in 2018 began including the 1% minimum portion of the Consolidated Revenue Fund—amounting to 55 billion naira in 2018 – to fund the BHCPF. The Fund is designed to deliver a guaranteed set health services to all Nigerians, through the national network of Primary Health Care centres.

- Passage of enabling legislation for the Nigeria Centre for Disease Control (NCDC), for the first time since it was founded in 2011. President Buhari approved a grant of 5 billion naira for the NCDC in March 2020, as part of the response to the Coronavirus pandemic.

- Tertiary Healthcare Upgrade Programme: A number of key Federal Hospitals across the country are being upgraded to effectively manage cancer and other major health challenges. Cancer Radiotherapy machines and other equipment are being provided to these hospitals. The National Hospital in Abuja has already received two LINAC (cancer treatment) machines.

- Nigeria Sovereign Investment Authority (NSIA) in March 2018 invested US $10 million to establish a world-class Cancer Treatment Centre at the Lagos University Teaching Hospital

(LUTH), and US $5 million each in the Aminu Kano University Teaching Hospital and the Federal Medical Centre, Umuahia, to establish modern Diagnostic Centres. These Centres have all been completed and are now operational.

- Launch in 2019 of a Cancer Treatment Support Programme, 'Chemotherapy Access Partnership', as a public-private partnership between the federal government of Nigeria and a Private Sector coalition, to enable Nigerian's access lower-cost, high-quality medications for the treatment of several types of cancer.

CONCLUSION

Who would have thought that little drops of water would form an ocean?

Similarly, who would have thought the small amounts of stealing and embezzling of government funds in Nigeria would have turned into this huge stealing of billions of naira?

Nigerian-corrupted behaviour is also comparable to a small fire that was not stopped when it first started. It burned out of control and has now turned into an uncontrollable wildfire burning dangerously. The flames have pervaded through every part of the nation. The wildfire has moved to the south, the west, the east, and the northern region of Nigeria. I do not see any region in Nigeria that the wildfire has not spread into. Wildfires are harmful and threatening to human beings, and they impact our landscaping. They are perilous to human welfare. So are the nefarious actions of Nigerians who steal in order to live luxuriously. These actions are no doubt an imminent danger that is hindering Nigeria from progressing and causing it to remain as an underdeveloped country to this day.

The rage, insecurity, and kidnappings that we are seeing today in Nigeria is a result of the pent-up anger and hatred toward the current situation. People are angry, furious, and seriously fed up with the people that are embezzling the funds and diverting it into their own personal bank accounts.

The Nigeria systems of political ruling are not based according to the principles or consideration of equality and justice, and the political leaders' practices are definitely inhumane and unjust too—extremely unfair.

To the leaders, politicians, and government appointees: if the roles were to be reversed, wouldn't you be furious and upset too? Close your eyes and imagine your children attending school and having to sit on the floor; no chairs for them to sit on or tables present for them to write on; your children having to do their assignments in the darkness, with little light present when they get home. Before you poke another person's skin with a needle, why don't you use the needle to poke your own skin first. "We must come to see that the end we seek is a society at peace with itself, a society that can live with its conscience."–Martin Luther King Jr. (KeepInspiring.me. n.d.).

"There comes a time when people get tired of being pushed out of the glittering sunlight of life's July and left standing amid the piercing chill of an alpine November."–Martin Luther King Jr. (KeepInspiring. me. n.d.).

The corruption has been allowed to go on for far too long in our nation. It's time to extinguish the fire that is burning through Nigeria right now. Nigerians, carry your extinguishers and say it as loud as you can: NO to the corrupted nature of Nigeria, and NO to stealing.

The time is now for us to start controlling this elusive and destructive behaviour sweeping through Nigeria and handling it peacefully.

"No one uses fire to fight fires, wins."

"That old law about 'an eye for an eye' leaves everybody blind. The time is always right to do the right thing."

"Love is the only force capable of transforming an enemy into friend."

"I believe that unarmed truth and unconditional love will have the final word in reality. This is why right, temporarily defeated, is stronger than evil triumphant."

—Martin Luther King Jr
(KeepInspiring.me. n.d.).

It's time we all collectively find the courage together to fight the corruption plaguing our nations. However, we must be peaceful in this fight. We will not win if we choose to fight or destroy properties. We should all learn from the above quotations by Martin Luther King Jr.— he had a dream, and he firmly believed peace should be the only way to achieve it. Nigerians should all share that same belief: corruptions will decrease in Nigeria if we go about trying to stop it peacefully.

Collectively, Nigerians need to go through the healing process of curbing corruptions. We shall get there, but remember that it will be a gradual process. The shift will not happen overnight. Riots and fights will only make the situation worse, and the issues will not be resolved.

Furthermore, when the bone of a child is curved (Scolosis), the best time to repair it and straighten it out is when the child is still growing up. This is because the bone is still flexible and not completely formed like it is as an adult. The corruption in Nigeria is comparable to the curvature of the spine that wasn't repaired as a child and now needs to be repaired in adulthood. It is going to be a difficult repair because the bone is already formed and much less flexible, but it is still possible. Similarly, fighting corruption that was not stopped when it first started will be difficult to stop now because it has eaten into the nation. However, it is still possible to fight it, especially with love rather than hate.

Some of our Nigerians do not know how to live in a structured nation, so they do not know how to ask for a structured nation or demand their rights. Most Nigerians only know of the unstructured, decaying Nigeria, and they have become too accustomed to be living that way.

What do I want you to take away after reading this? I want you to know that it's totally wrong to be silent and take on all of the pain, suffering, abuse, and humiliation without verbalizing the agony it is causing to our existence. Stealing, corruption, and embezzling public funds is causing the nation chaos and poverty.

It's tearing my heart apart to see that most of our Nigerians lack integrity in terms of responsibility, leadership, legacy, empathy, and accountability. Because of the greed for wealth and status, most Nigerian kids have had to live through being rejected from their families due to their lack of status and wealth. It is appalling to know that this is happening to our children. All humans matter whether they are wealthy or not; all of the children in the nation matter and need equal treatment.

Look around you—do you see what I see too? Politicians' actions and promises during their elections are not congruent with the services being delivered once they're elected. Nigerians, you need to know that you do not have to accept this. Shout out, "NO!" and let your voice be heard. Your voice counts, and your voice matters. You have rights that need to be upheld. You should not allow any politicians to use you as a thug to fight their elections for them. Some of you will get wounded or even killed. Where are the kids of these politicians? They're living abroad and attending school with the money that has been stolen from public funds. Some of their kids are living in Nigeria, chilling in mansions that have been built with our public money. Where are you kids going to school? That is, even if your parents can afford to send you to school. You people get schooled in rundown buildings and live in underdeveloped houses. I want you guys to think. Think, guys!

Yoruba says, "ori ko ju ori."

This means that one head is not bigger than the other. A more literal translation explains it as, "We are all equal." Rich or poor, we are all equal.

"We must build dikes of courage to hold back the flood of fear."—Martin Luther King Jr. (KeepInspiring.me. n.d.).

When next you are approached to be a thug, to fight and destroy the right candidates, I want you to remember my words in this book and say, "No!" Fighting the right candidates means you have just destroyed your own future and your children's future.

To paraphrase Martin Luther King Jr.—"All we say to [Nigeria] is, 'Be true to what you said on paper.'... But somewhere I read of the freedom of assembly. Somewhere I read of the freedom of speech. Somewhere I read of the freedom of the press. Somewhere I read that the [giant of Africa] is the right to protest for right" (KeepInspiring.me. n.d.).

Nigeria needs a time machine to turn the clock backward, to travel to the past to when things were right and begin again from that point. Going back, it is possible to find solutions in general relativity that will allow Nigeria to be rebuilt to its old glorious days known as the African Giant.

Nigerians, what shifts would you like to see? How do you think you can get to the shifts? What are your inputs to these shifts?

The shift will not happen if we all don't work hard with love to achieve the dreams we are all reaching for.

I am praying and seeking for it to happen. What would you all like to see happen?

The political and religious supremacy with the ambitions of wealth have ruined the vibrant nation. The corruption has deprived many Nigerians from achieving their dreams, goals, and the ability to provide for their children or families.

There is no peace in the nation because opportunities are not equally distributed, which is shattering. Our people are boiling from intense anger that is building due to the social injustice still taking place. Our people continue to endure the devastating corruption. Intervention is a necessity at this stage.

Oh our home, oh our Nigerians Arise, oh compatriots, oh when do we serve with our hearts, without selfishness, with considerations, when shall we obey our land, when shall we see our Native Nigeria land developed and be great again. We shall never forget how it used to be great. We had good roads, constant electricity, good drinking water, good quality schools, free education, and one of the best healthcare systems (University Teaching Hospital in Ibadan). We had quality infrastructure, a booming agriculture industry, security throughout the entire nation, and we were free of corruption. We had justice, peace, happiness, and prosperity reigning in the land. Nigerians will never forget how this nation used to be so great.

We must break the shady diversion of public funds into personal use, which is extremely common and affecting the quality of our humanity. Extreme situations demand extreme reactions. The country needs extreme strategic actions such as an executive order to curb and end corruption and the stealing of public funds. This will show consideration for the needs and concerns of other people; that will be very thoughtful. It's fundamentally dangerous not to; the group that it's affecting mostly are our children, and they are playing with the future of our children lives. This is what is needed—we need something that will serve as a deterrent to others, something that will make them stop. It's not right, and it's surely not fair.

Who is with me? It's time we collectively stand our ground to combat and "stop the stealing and corruptions act." One way or the other, corruption needs to be addressed. Stop treating us with prejudice in our father's land because you hold a position of power—it's injustice.

Nigerians are at the point that we have to confront the truth; let's face the facts and call a spade a spade.

To all political leaders at all levels of government that have ruled the country, you have all failed woefully, on a scale of 0 to10, your score is 1; look around yourself.

Look at the pictures following.

Is this the state in which we are going to leave the country for our children and their children?

Come on now, people.

Okereke I. (2019 August 14). "inside plateau primary schools where pupils learn under trees in dilapidated structures". Premium Times.

Dahiru A. (2020 October 13). "Abuja community cries over dilapidated classes as schools resume". HumAngle.

Etim E. (2018, July 4) "Dilapidated schools in Akwa Ibom". Guardian Opinion

Zik G. (2020 February 18). Students still learning on bare floors in Delta state schools. Reformer.

REFERENCES

Acosta O. and Gonzalez J. I (2010). "A thermodynamic approach for emergence of globalization ", in Deng K.G.(ed) Globalization - Today, Tomorrow. Croatia: Sciyo.

Adjibolosoo, S.(2007) "Creating an Integrated Vehicle for Global Participation and Gain - sharing ". Paper prepared for the Free Market Forum," The role of Markets and Government in Pursuing the Common Good." Panel Topic: Globalization and the Common Good of Hillsdale College, September 29.

Ayough Samuel, Research Report on Trends in African Countries, Military Factions, 1978, Nigeria.

Blackpast. 2009. (1957) ABUBAKAR TAFAWA BALEWA, "FIRST SPEECH AS PRIME MINISTER". Blackpast. August 20. https://www.blackpast.org/global-african-history/1957-abubakar-tafawa-balewa-first-speech-prime-minister/.

Dogara, G.N. " Impact of Globalization in Nigeria", Ph.D Thesis, Department of Business Administration, Nasarawa State University, Nigeria, Published by European Centre for Business Training and Development, UK, Vol 3, No4, pp 36, May, 2015.

Eregha, P. B. and Irughe I. R.(2009). Oil Induced Environmental Degradation in the Nigeria's Niger Delta: The Multiplier Effects," Journal of Sustainable Development in Africa, 11(4).

George Simmel, Conflict and the Web of Group Affiliation. Translated by K. Wolf and R. Bendic, New York. The Free press, 1955.

Giddens, A. (1990). The Consequences of Modernity. Cambridge: polity Press

Henry Bienen, Harnessing the ideas of Lenin, Moa, and Debray about Violence to a Concept of Social Change in, Violence and Social Change. Chicago, 1968.

Holsti, K.J. International Politics: A Framework for Analysis. Prentice Hall Inc. New Jersey, 1972.

Idowu, Bolaji, African Traditional Religion. Fountain Publication, Ibadan, 1991.

ILO, (2001), Stopping Forced Labour: Global report under the follow - up to the ILO Declaration on Fundamental Principles and Rights at Work, International Labour Conference, 89th Session 2001, Report 1B.

Iyayi, F. (2004) "Globalization, The Nigerian Economy and Peace" in Akani, C. Globalization and the Peoples of Africa, Enugu: Fourth Dimension Publishing Ltd.

Jaja, J. M. (2010). " Globalization or Americanization: Implications for Sub - Saharan Africa", in Deng K. G.(ed) Globalization - Today, Tomorrow. Croatia: Sciyo.

John 8:4-11 NIV - - Bible Gateway, https://www.biblegateway.com/ passage/?search=John%2B8%3A4-11&version=NIV.

John Dollard et al (ed) Frustration and Aggression, New Haven. Yale University Press, 1939.

John Locke. Of Civil Government, London: Cassel and Co. 1901. Class Relations and Racial Discrimination in South Africa, Routledge and Kegan Paul, London, 1976.

Karl W. Deutsih, " Social Mobilization and Political Development" APSR, 55.3 (Sept.1961) reprinted in Gason L. Finkle and Richard W. Gable(ed) Political Development and Social Change 2nd (Ed) New York, John Wiley and Sons, 1971.

KeepInspiring.me. n.d. "Abraham Lincoln Quotes." https://www.keep-inspiring.me/abraham-lincoln-quotes/#more-2702.

KeepInspiring.me. n.d. "Martin Luther King Jr Quotes." https://www.keepinspiring.me/martin-luther-king-jr-quotes/.

Matthew 22:37-39 NIV - - Bible Gateway, https://www.biblegateway.com/passage/?search=Matthew+22%3A37-39&version=NIV.

Nigeria High Commission. n.d. "Nigerian National Anthem." http://www.nigeriahc.org.uk/national-anthem.

Nigeria High Commission. n.d. "National Pledge." http://www.nigeriahc.org.uk/national-anthem.

Nwankwo A., Civilianized Soldiers: Army Civilian Government for Nigeria. Fourth Dimension Publishers, Enugu, Nigeria, 1984.

Okwudibia, Nnoli, Ethnic Politics in Nigeria. Fourth Dimension Publishers, Enugu, Nigeria, 1980.

Oyeleye Oyedina (ed) Nigerian Government and Politics Under Military Rule, DUP, 1979.

Papke, David R. 2015. KARL MARX ON RELIGION. January 20. https://law.marquette.edu/facultyblog/2015/01/karl-marx-on-religion/comment-page-1/#:~:text=Marx's%20actual%20words%20regarding%20religion,soul%20of%20our%20soulless%20conditions.%E2%80%9D

Talcott Parsons. The Social System. New York, the Free Press, 1951.

PM Store Author's QR Code

https://pagemasterpublishing.ca/by/christine-umoekereka/

To order more copies of this book, find books by other
Canadian authors, or make inquiries about publishing
your own book, contact PageMaster at:

PageMaster Publication Services Inc.
11340-120 Street, Edmonton, AB T5G 0W5
books@pagemaster.ca
780-425-9303

catalogue and e-commerce store
PageMasterPublishing.ca/Shop

ABOUT THE AUTHOR

Christine Umoekereka (Shutti) is a Nigerian-born healthcare professional based in Canada who has practised nursing for over twenty years. Due to her love, passion, and commitment to her work over the years, she has been able to touch the lives of many people both at home and abroad. She is seen as a valuable and committed professional in her field, and many of her patients have acknowledged the positive impact of her dedication to her job.

Despite the fact that she is not living in Nigeria and has lived in the developed world for many years, Christine is a philanthropist and a patriotic Nigerian who is passionate about the well-being and development of her country. Her passion to see Nigeria as one of the most developed, corruption-free countries in the world has propelled her to embark on a philanthropic journey that has led her to spend thousands of dollars in collaboration with the Local Government Education Authority, Agege, Lagos State, Nigeria on free health training for parents, teachers, non-academic staff, and other stakeholders in the Agege Local Government Area in 2015. The training attracted over 2000 participants from around Lagos State. Today, Christine is one of the advocates of change in a different sphere of life.

Her passion for a better and prosperous Nigeria led her into putting this book together to address some major challenges in Nigeria, and how collectively we can change things for the betterment of her beloved country—where fairness, equality, and considerations for peace and justice may reign.

Pastor Michael Success Abuja